DID YOU SEE THE ELEPH/

1950's life remembered

By

Kevin Dewane
2020

Throughout my life with my Nana,when she was bringing me up,every day was sprinkled with sayings,phrases and idioms which she used to make one point or another.At any time day or night these little snippets would surface,some very simple some more complex but each able to make a valid point.As always their randomness was part of the attraction so look out for them during the following memories.Some you may have heard of some maybe not,so lets see when they appear what memories they may possibly invoke from your past,when,where and why they were used and by whom.

"There's many a slip twixt the cup and the lip"

****

It was a fine sunny day,just the opportunity for us to head towards Gosport High Street at a leisurely pace,it was nice to walk and we started off with a spring in our step.Passing the junction with Norman Road we had to stop to make way for one of Treloars,the demolition contractors,big blue and grey Thames Trader tipper trucks as it turned out of the demolition yard,heading towards its destination via Leesland Road.As it noisily turned the corner it was a very different sound to that we had heard from this spot on Sunday when the Salvation Army band,resplendent in their black and maroon uniforms with peaked caps and bonnets,treated us to renditions of popular hymns accompanied by an enthusiastic choir.They had marched from their hall at the Crossways,situated opposite a block of public conveniences that stood by the bus stop,the brass and silver instruments booming out rousing tunes in the hope of attracting new recruits to"the army of God".On Sundays my Nana would hurry me past,classing them almost as blasphemers due to their brand of christianity, I was fascinated by the band, most small boys were but I was not allowed to pause.Their main source of revenue was from the sale of"The Warcry",a paper which they sold in public houses as they were of the temperance persuasion seeing people who drank alcohol as fallen sinners.

Today as we marched alongside ourselves,we soon arrived at Lees Lane railway crossing,where old Percy manned the wooden signal box.Over the level crossing into Lees Lane I gazed at Ashleys,the wallpaper factory with its tall chimney,on the opposite side of the road to the old Forton Prison which was now houses having been demolished before the war.Passing on we encountered "The Dugout",a little sweet shop in the middle of a terrace of houses before eventually finding ourselves arriving at a fork in the road,on the island between the two forks stood"the fleapit",its real name The Criterion cinema which even then had seen

2

better days.Taking the right hand fork we came out on Forton Road,which led to the main town centre passing St John's Church and Eddie Crosslands funeral directors,Eddie a man whose services our family had cause to use many times over the years in less happy circumstances.Forton Road was a road of some length as it also ran the opposite direction from which we were going up to its junction with Anns Hill Road,our route taking us down to St Georges Barracks and Clarence Square.Today we were heading down towards the railway station which was the end of the line for all but military personnel.Forton Road ran parallel to the railway line,which passed behind the barbers shop where Nana took me for my"short back and sides",on a Friday afternoon, when school had finished,its final stop the Victorian station.There were still plenty of empty and weed strewn bomb sites around us,reminders of the war years,these sprouted purple buddleia,yellow ragwort and mauve michaelmas daisies where they still lingered unloved,the natural world desperate to hide them,but starkly visible on the corners of Moreland Road and Mill Lane.As we crossed Mill Lane the barrack buildings of St Vincent naval training establishment appeared on our left, on the opposite of the road the playing fields used by the cadets who lived in its dormitories.I stopped and peered through the entrance gates hoping to catch a glimpse of the cadets practicing their ceremony of "manning the mast",but today it was not to be the parade ground was empty.

****

"A stitch in time saves nine"

****

Walking briskly along towards the White Swan public house on the corner of Ferrol Road,I loved to pause and look at the BSA,Triumph,AJS and Norton motorbikes that stood at the kerbside outside the front of Everetts motorbike showrooms.On the opposite corner to the public house stood a small rather nondescript petrol station.Crossing the road that ran down the side of it,Parham Road,on the corner stood the imposing facade of the warehouse building and offices of I.K.C.,Ivens Kellets and Childs,badly damaged in the war before once again being returned to its former glory.Now it stood filled with the groceries waiting to be loaded onto the orange and brown lorries which would take them to the local corner stores and grocers shops.

Most of the bombs that fell on it during the wartime period were in fact directed at the oil tanks which stood adjacent to it,they themselves standing behind a vast concrete wall and buried in huge grass and earth embankments,providing a vital supply line to the Royal Navy's contribution to the war effort.The black painted oil storage tanks still stood in use,the entrance to them being behind extremely high grey wooden gates.On the opposite side of the road The Railway Tavern provided accommodation and refreshments for the railway passengers,until the trains ran no more,other than to supply goods,a few yards past,the railway lines crossed the road from Gosport's Victorian railway station into the entrance of the fuel dump where a military railway would transport fuel oil to the dockside,along with other provisions.The lovely pillared front of the Victorian Railway station, which had many times played host to Queen Victoria herself when she was travelling to Stokes Bay, on her way to Osborne House in the Isle of Wight was starting to fall into disrepair.Weeds and small bushes which had self set were beginning to grow between the railway tracks and even out of the top ledges of the station itself.Only goods wagons and steam engines,gradually being replaced by diesel engines,echoed in the booking hall,trains with no more passengers to transport were at the end of the line.A small diesel shunting engine pushed or pulled the wagons across Forton Road,through the level crossing gates,then the narrow tunnel leading into Clarence Yard.As we passed this we skirted around the parapets of the little tunnel to come to the balustraded portico of Clarence Yard,one of the victualling yards for the navy.Coming out of the entrance was a short slightly stout middle aged man,he had a ruddy round face topped with a shock of white curly hair,black framed glasses perched on his nose and he walked with a slight roll in his gait."Hello Annie" he said in a soft lilting Irish accent."Hello Tom how are you" she countered,turning to me she said"this is your Uncle Tom,say hello".Dutifully I greeted this friendly looking man,having no idea really who he was,finding out later that he was my grandfather's brother on my dads branch of the family.When my Nana had said her farewells to the friendly man,I politely said"Goodbye" and when we were out of earshot asked as,we walked on past the barracks,"who was that man','That was Grandad Dewane's brother Tom",she replied,he works there and knows your dad,curiosity satisfied I was to see the man on several more occasions after that as we passed the yard and I would always be cheerfully greeted.

****

"He's a chip off of the old block"

****

After the end of the second world war Victorian values and the Church of England still played a large part shaping our lives and acceptable behaviour,consequently the church and its teachings had become a huge influence on everyday living.It was important to follow their doctrines and to be baptised,it was important"to believe in God"and this mantra was instilled in a child from the very time they were born,whenever I misbehaved I would be rebuked with the words"God Is watching you".At home I would be expected to kneel and say my prayers every night before getting into bed,thanking God for the day I had enjoyed,asking him for a favourable day for me and every other family member the next day.At mealtimes"grace" was said before we ate anything."For what we are about to receive may the Lord make us truly thankful" became second nature at every mealtime.I was taught even before I had started primary school how to recite The Lord's Prayer,every assembly,every morning,when I started school involved it being recited out loud.,Leesland school was after all a Church of England school its foundation firmly based on religious and spiritual beliefs and teachings..Religious festivals,Easter,Christmas and Ascension Day it was normal for me to march,two by two with my teachers to St Faiths Church in order to observe these important dates in the church calendar.Churches on Sundays had huge congregations,the streets busier then than during the weekdays,everyone dressed in their"Sunday best" to look acceptable in the "face of God",my Nana attended every week,rain or shine,healthy or sick, harvest suppers,fetes,and garden parties were all well attended and were significant in the infrastructure of the local community.Christening was seen as an important start in a newborn disciples path in life,birthdays saw me given a prayer book and a bible, and as I became older it was imperative that I was confirmed into the church,so I"could participate in full"by partaking of Holy Communion.Sunday school took you through religious teachings as you were prepared for what was seen as"the big day in your life",on confirmation day I was given a crucifix on a chain as a confirmation present,a constant reminder of my "faith".The local vicar was seen as a person to be revered,the fount of all wisdom,a person to give you advice and guidance in even your personal and private life,known by everyone in the parish,someone you could approach for help and advice.Churchyards,old or new, and neatly tended cemeteries were places of contemplation and tranquility,you didn't walk on the grassy graves,you treated them with the respect for the person interred beneath them,peace and silence were all part of the religious pathway in our lives.Even in death it was still quite normal for the corpse to be laid out in the parlour of their house,not only so the body departed on its journey to the final resting place from its home,but also so that neighbours and friends could pray at the coffin as they paid their last respects.As the cortege departed,curtains in the houses were drawn shut,people removed any headwear,bowed their heads and crossed their chests,silently muttering "rest in peace". There were strict behaviours many of which evolved from what the church dictated,but importantly it did give some form of structure to our everyday lives in a situation that was still recovering from five years of wartime upheaval.

****

"A bird in the hand is worth two in the bush"

****

Summers seemed to be so very different,slower,no rushing,little noise,you could hear birds singing,we walked everywhere or boarded a bus,cars were an expensive luxury that few could afford and with a young family it was extremely hard,harder still if you were an old age pensioner.Days,or rather afternoons,as womenfolk were expected to do their housework in the mornings,were the time when you saw mothers and their families heading towards the beach.To get to the beach was,with a gaggle of grizzly children,a bit of a logistical nightmare,coping with a four year old,my sister,and the pushchair loaded with toys,games and food for tea,Nana,already of pensionable age felt,and appeared more like an overworked packhorse.On the route to Stokes Bay it wasn't too bad as the pushchair was used as a means to carry the luggage,but coming back when I was too tired to walk so it wasn't quite so easy.A grizzly child did not "settle" too happily on an uncomfortable seat,made up of all the things we had taken with us,along with the stones and shells we had collected whilst there,the situation was not improved either, by the moaning of my sister who was forced to help carry some of the luggage.The outward journey led down Anns Hill Road,past the police box on the corner of The Avenue,before continuing along Jellicoe Avenue,into Western Way to the entrance into Stanley Park.Excitedly I ran on ahead,making sure I never went out of Nana's sight,although there was little to fear, just continuously skipping,singing and running back and forwards.I couldn't get to the beach quickly enough,oblivious of the fact that everyone else was melting in the heat,I continued to ran ahead across Stanley Park whilst they endeavoured to catch me up.I eventually arrived at an enormous prehistoric monkey puzzle tree with leaves like armour,it towered above the other trees and people said no animals populate it because of the leaves,but to me it was a constant source of fascination.Nana's voice could be heard frequently shouting"keep of the grass",although small white metal signs on the closely mown lawns were a constant reminder to us to do exactly that."Wait for us" she cried as I continued running ahead,once again,and when I ignored the comment she would say"so you don't want an ice cream then".Of course I did,it was guaranteed to stop me in my tracks,so I waited,then walked with her as we went to the little open window at the rear of the Alverbank hotel to buy a small ice cream cornet.As ice cream dribbled down my chin,the hot air melting it before I could eat it,Nana would periodically spit on her clean handkerchief and wipe off the offending residue as we walked down the footpath and over the bridge crossing the algae strewn moat,then across the road onto the stony but inviting beach.

Once arrived on the shingle covered beach,bath towels and tartan travel rugs were lain on the expanse of pebbles,carefully checking as we went that there were no tar deposits or prickly sea holly plants in the way.It was at last time to have a dip in the sea.In todays world we must have looked like characters from a silent movie comedy,Nana with her skirt hitched up,suitably dressed in a hat and blouse,Grandad with his trousers rolled up to the knees,cigarette between his stained yellowing teeth,newspaper under his arm and a clean handkerchief knotted in the four corners to make a head covering.My sister and I fared no better in the swimwear of the day,hers a one piece affair covering almost all of her skin and me,with a white sun hat and a pair of knitted,yes knitted in wool,swimming trunks which once wet had disastrous results,the weight of the water stretching them down to my feet,resulting at times in leaving little to the imagination.Exiting the water we dried off,desperately hiding our modesty behind a bath towel,struggling to get your pants and knickers on in a manner that fellow beach goers"mustn't see"your private parts."Swim" over we were ready at last to tuck in to the sandwiches and cake which were now,in the heat,turning rather desiccated and curling at the edges,greaseproof paper really did very little to keep them fresh,The homemade lemonade was now warm and the milk in the flask of tea"tasted funny",probably because it was already"on the turn" when it had been originally put in,needless to say as there was nothing else we had to make do.Why I still can't comprehend did we sit on an open beach with no shade in rising temperatures,fully dressed,trying in any conceivable way to avoid the sun at all costs,it seemingly being unimaginable to show too much of the body as it was impolite,even rude to be in a state of such" undress'

****

"There bark is worse than their bite"

****

By the end of the 1950's things were beginning to change,technology was starting to gather pace and I remember items around me beginning to gradually start to change too,slowly at first but then accelerating sharply.Wages had started to rise,mass production increased the availability of products,at the same time making them cheaper to purchase and credit meant people could borrow money and not have to save to make a purchase.Instead off you buying only what you had the money saved up for,you spent it before you had even earned it.Waiting became a thing of the past,items became"must haves"and many of the old sayings we lived by lost their relevance. Grandad would sit and read his copy of the weekly"John Bull",puffing a very thin rollup and supping his ever favourite milk stout,constantly foretelling what was going to happen in the future and now sixty years after his death I am afraid to say he was not far from the truth.A huge "stereo unit"by Grundig replaced the sideboard,portable transistor radios,the size of a breeze block with huge tuning dials replaced the old valve radios.Tape recorders and Zoom 8 cine cameras recorded sound and movement,home movies were the thing of the future,but they weren't.Electricity in every house was to become normal,replacing the gas, but still prepayment by meter was the preferred method to pay.Telephones were the must have item,mostly connected on party lines,it was cheaper,the disadvantage was that your neighbour who shared your line could listen to your conversation.If you needed 999 and they were using their phone you would have to go and ask them to hang up.Smoking was widely accepted,actively encouraged even by the family doctor, and quite often we would club together and waylay a passing stranger,the age for smoking was sixteen,to buy us five Park Drive or even a single cigarette for a penny.Trendy teenagers thought it was "cool" to smoke and would aspire to have a Mobylette moped and these, as motorbikes, were largely ridden without crash helmets,cars similarly devoid of seatbelts,neither the subject of motoring legislature at the time.The kitchen copper became a twin tub washing machine,linoleum was replaced with Axminster or Wilton wool carpets.Outside privies made way for indoor toilets,the zinc bath was replaced with a bathroom with hot and cold running water.At the same time radiators began to replace coal fires as the prime source of heating.The refrigerator replaced the meat safe on the wall of the backyard and the bucket of water to keep the milk fresh,the freezer compartment,in the fridge, stored frozen food,in fact only really ice cream.The mangle was about to be replaced by the tumble dryer,shaving became electric,replacing the shaving soap and badger hair brush.As coal fires disappeared flat irons became electric,electric toasters saw the demise of the toasting fork,the toast however was far less flavoursome.Hoovers replaced brooms,hair dryers replaced towels,bed lamps replaced candles the list was endless.

****

"Don't jump out of the frying pan into the fire"

****

All around as we moved forward old values and close associations with neighbours became more fragmented.As people wanted more,quicker ways were found to produce more and old ways and traditions began to disappear.The delivery drivers with horse and carts replaced them with electric vehicles, but as these tended to be slow they soon progressed to petrol and diesel vehicles.At the farms tractors and combine harvesters replaced the faithful shire horses,grass cutters towed by tractors replaced scythe and sickle.Silver milk churns that stood at the farm gates waiting to be collected by a lorry were no longer needed as the milk was pumped into a tanker lorry.Tradesmen and shop owners saw changes everywhere.Mr Jones the butcher had an electric bandsaw to replace the traditional handsaw.The cobbler saw stick on rubber soles replace his shoe repair skills.Even when we went to meet our maker we were no longer always buried but found ourselves in a crematorium,soon the skilled gravedigger would lose his job to a mechanical competitor,not better but quicker.Groceries became prepacked replacing the ability to purchase just what you needed,prepacked supposedly meant cheaper,practically it increased wastage and took away people's ability to need to plan their shopping.All of these small changes and there were many, gradually crept in,almost unnoticed and in the twenty first century have left us trying desperately to solve a problem that these actions have catastrophically created.

****

''The pot calling the kettle black''

****

It was that unforgettable kind of dawn,fingers of golden sunlight gradually lighting up the quiet street as the sun rose over the horizon, and by the time we had eaten our breakfast there were signs of that oppressive sticky heat that would only increase as the sultry day wore on.It was getting humid already,shorts and short sleeved shirt were the best clothes for the day and even then you would still sweat profusely.Playing on the pavement outside number 80 Leesland Road,I was accompanied by the first emerging flying ants which were preparing to swarm at the end of the day, when they would tangle themselves in my hair and clothes.It was still only early morning but already it was too hot to be anything but sedentary,it was the school holidays but how was I going to keep cool enough to do anything,football was out of the question,so was cricket,so by lunchtime a languid listless mood had set in.Really it was weather for being near water,even better playing in it,either sea,lake,river,lido or swimming pool,but everyone was busy doing other more important things,nobody was available to go with me.At this point enter Grandad,dear old grandad,a man of few words but reliable,kind and very hardworking.He was a dour man,had a smug cheeky grin,smiling eyes,yellowing teeth and a long wisp of grey hair,combed over his otherwise bald head,rarely seen as it was concealed under the flat cap he constantly wore.Fresh from his daily pint of bitter at The Junction public house,his dinner was on the table as he walked over the doorstep through the front door,he was"as regular as clockwork",but in those times everyone was "on time".As he entered the door,washed his hands and sat down to eat, he told Nana of his intention to spend the afternoon at the family allotment in Middlecroft Lane,it possible to enter by a gate the garden of 16 Oxford Road.Did she want any vegetables brought back he asked. My ears pricked up,"can I come I asked","I'm not sure it's very hot"replied Grandad,"the boy can't do any harm it wouldn't hurt"said Nana and reluctantly Grandad acquiesced,giving me a coy,slightly reproachful glance as if he would rather I didn't go,knowing from experience how easily I became bored.My excitement knew no bounds,my patience was not a known quality and today was no exception,he knew only too well from previous occasions that he would find it hard to keep me occupied for two or three hours. Grandad's after dinner "nap" that day was constantly interrupted by "are you ready yet,aww come on grandad".Slowly worn down eventually an invitation of,"oh come on then", more cussed than uttered, saw us venture forth together up a deserted hot dusty Leesland Road.Grandad carried a long handled hoe, which he had taken home to sharpen the week before and I carried a wooden trug to carry our produce back home later.From Anns Hill Road we walked down the road at the side of the arch into Middlecroft Lane,passed the uninviting Middlecroft public house,then onto a dusty,stoney track leading to the allotments.All in neat straight rows tidy,weed free,even the large stones removed to leave a fine tilth clear evidence of the pride that gardeners had in their little vegetable plots.Entering through an ungated entrance,up a well kept path,once I arrived at our allotment I headed towards a sheet of old rusty corrugated tin laying on the grass path,in the hope of finding a grass snake or slow worm.Butterflies,red admiral,peacocks and tortoiseshell were flying like jewels around the flowers but it was mostly cabbage white butterflies,that laid their little white eggs in clusters under the leaves of newly planted brassicas that were most abundant.Some eggs had already hatched out into green caterpillars,ravenous little pests that munched holes in the cabbage leaves,all of which were picked off and thrown to the attentive robin redbreast.Around the edge of the allotment were fruiting Lord Lambourn,Charles Ross and Granny Smith apple trees,in the neat rows on the allotment itself grew peas,onions,beans and potatoes, Kelvedon Wonder,Ailsa Craig,Aquadulce,Arran Comet,Pentland Javelin,all old vegetable varieties no longer seen as being commercially viable in today's modern life.Tired,completely exhausted from the heat,sweating even from the smallest efforts I had made,all I wanted to do was sit in the shade but my job was still to be done and it did help in cooling me down.I dipped the watering can into a reservoir of green stagnant water, stored in an old zinc water tank recycled from a bombed out house from the recent war.The idea was to create a fine spray of water from a rose on the end of the can's spout,with no rose to get a fine spray it was down to ingenuity and a hosepipe.Using my thumb to partially block the flow from the hosepipe,I could clumsily obtain the same result apart from myself becoming unduly wetter than normal in the process.At last I finished the watering so helped Grandad to collect Nana's fruit and vegetable requirements,not without reward,as a proportion of the soft fruit never saw the trug but went towards refreshing my dry mouth.Having finished picking the required items,we wearily carried the overflowing trug of blackcurrants and   redcurrants,gooseberries,strawberries,peas and broad beans and slowly wandered back down Southcroft Road in time for tea.

****

''Every cloud has a silver lining''

****

After having been at Leesland School for a couple of weeks like all the boys I soon became involved with playing football,mostly in the little playground at break times.Cigarette and tea cards,given free in the cardboard packets portrayed our heroes and the popular teams of the era, helped by the pictures that were free in these various packets,we would pick our teams, pretending to be a star player for the team we supported,Manchester United,Arsenal,Liverpool and Wolverhampton Wanderers,a few years later our lunchtime was shattered by the news of the Munich air disaster and the loss of many talented footballers.I remember sitting in front of the coal fire at Nanas on a bitterly cold day in that March of 1958 and the tears in my eyes when the news broke on the radio.Nana and Grandad sat in horror,shock and sadness as the news of the casualties were revealed,Manchester United's young players were known to everyone.Our local team was Portsmouth but most of my friends supported the ''glamour clubs'' in fact the ones in the headlines at the time,it was a matter of supporting a team that was winning at the,Liverpool,Leeds,WolverhamptonWanderers,Arsenal and Tottenham.After that day I followed United,but Portsmouth still lured me to their cold draughty terraces at Fratton Park when I was old enough to attend a football match.Six years later at the same time,in the same place those tears were shed again at the news of the deaths of so may children at Aberfan school.Several years later I preferred to play rugby, probably because my physique was more suitable,but for now it was football.We would play a ''game'' with anything that resembled a ball,it could be with a stone,shoe,tin can,conker,tennis ball and occasionally an actual football.During lunch and midmorning and afternoon breaks,we used piles of jumpers as goal posts,on pitches with no boundaries.The official game refereed by one of the teachers used to be played on the grass the opposite side of Daisy Lane which was the Central School playing field,the same place that was used in the summer for the annual school sports days.On that day parents turned up on a summer's afternoon looking forward eagerly to see their precious child hopefully win a prize,it was a carnival style atmosphere as the best athletes performed in a number of "athletic races",egg and spoon,wheelbarrow,sack and three legged races all necessary to prepare us should we ever attain the heights of Olympic competition.The array of sun hats,many just a white hankie knotted in each corner to form a cover to prevent Dad or Grandad's balding head from burning were supplemented by some elaborate cheap sunglasses certainly not prescribed by the school optician,many of those glasses were just a wire frame with two lenses from the NHS.My friends and I had anticipated the day for weeks but it was over in a flash,unless you were good enough to take part in the inter school games at the "stadium" in Privet Park.Otherwise it was just that one day,when we returned after the summer holidays these summer times were in the distant past and the new term was all about playing football once more.

****

"Look after the pennies,the pounds will look after themselves"

****

We had been back at school for a couple of weeks when one Friday evening after school Nana was waiting at the school gates,I had anticipated this evening all afternoon,in fact all week and now I was Skipping ahead down Daisy Lane on my way to Stokes Road.We passed the alleyway which led to Bury Crescent and my friend and his mother parted company with us to make their way home.As we continued on we passed the little grocers on the corner of the lane,where a few years later I had my first job cleaning up the backyard on a Saturday morning for half a crown,all at the tender age of ten.I ran on ahead,before turning down St Edwards Road at the bottom of which we would join up with Stoke Road which was the our destination.Briskly walking towards the town we passed the Forum Cinema,where I had seen my first film with Nana,"The Ten Commandments",next was Bull's hardware shop which appeared to sell everything, Pyles cake shop,the female staff dressed in brown check uniform with brown headwear,W H Smiths,newsagents with its row of red bicycles waiting for their paper boys,before eventually arriving outside the shop window of Nobes.The shop was full of sports items and I was here to buy my first pair of football boots,seemingly at the time styled on a pair of army boots.The idea was that they would make it easier to play in,giving better grip on muddy,wet,slippery fields but like with anything else it came at a cost.The boots were all made of brown leather with reinforced toe caps,fastened with about twenty feet of laces which you wrapped around your ankle and under the boot to secure them to your foot.In turn they stood on leather studs which were nailed into the boot,the nails often finding the sole of your foot when they came through the sole.Once the thick woollen socks were put on their was some protection.In the rain the boots became extremely heavy as did the laced leather ball,both getting stuck in the mud as the pitch turned to something akin to a ploughed field.The heavy ball was almost impossible to cross when wet and if you were unlucky enough to head it concussion was a likely outcome.The actual kit,itself,didn't help much either,the heavy cotton shirts with long sleeves,the long knee length shorts and if you were a goalkeeper a woollen jumper,which when wet impeded any jumping capability you had,all conspired to obstruct your efforts.There was a plus side,however, as it did keep you fairly warm when you turned up to play mid afternoon to find you were playing on a pitch that had not thawed out and was still frozen solid from the night before.Any thought of danger or broken legs never crossed my mind,frozen pitches,even those totally hidden by snow rarely stopped a game,you just got hold of a shovel and cleared the white lines ,you would just turn up and play along with your school friends or opponents.As I left the shop to wait outside,whilst Nana paid,I peered into the shop window,here the items needed to play a variety of sports were displayed.I looked longingly at the best of their day,wooden Slazenger and Dunlop tennis rackets strung with catgut and kept in shape with wooden racket presses.Heavy leather rugby balls with protective leather head guards with buckle fixings which were just as dangerous to wear as not to be using them.Shuttlecocks were cork and goose feather,darts had feather flights,tennis balls were only white,cricket balls only red.The cricket bats were endorsed by Wallie Hammond or Stuart Surridge,famous cricketers from the past.Football shirts were just numbered,if even that,many just plain white,red,green or blue,a few striped ones, shorts,black or white were tied up with cord around your waist.By now Nana had joined me,I briefly pointed out a leather football which was greeted with,"yes very nice,but another day,maybe at Christmas or your birthday, we must get home for tea now",looking back longingly I respectfully obeyed the instruction and followed dutifully,it wasn't too bad really I did have my new boots to christen at the next opportunity.

****

"Sticks and stones can break my bones but names will never hurt you"

September soon yielded to October,the football season had been in full swing for a little while and with the football came the inevitable football results.Friday nights as it became dark a knock would come on the door.Opening the door, on the pavement outside stood a man with a satchel slung over one shoulder,grasping a sheaf of papers in his other
hand."Hello Gerry" he would say as dad came to the door behind me."It's the pools man" I shouted."I'll just get it" said dad as I stood nervously shifting from foot to foot,coyly eyeing up the man standing outside.The evening was a fine one but on some evenings the man from Littlewoods or Vernons football pools would arrive looking like a drowned rat,whatever the weather he had to collect them and get them onto the overnight mail train to Liverpool.They had to arrive before Saturday,at midday,or else they wouldn't be included in the competition.A coupon was exchanged"new for old"the one filled in with crosses,trying to predict the results of the next day's football matches,accompanied with stake money placed into the hands of the pool's man,the unmarked coupon going the other way before it was marked up and put aside until the whole process took place again the following week.Whether it was one line or more,the stakes were placed in pennies, shillings,sometimes farthings,the possible rewards if you managed to pick eight draws on one line could be a win of several thousands of pounds.Inevitably it was unlikely but,Archie and Lofty Shepherd,two of dad's oldest friends, along with dad, did have one substantial win.A win which left him with a bungalow and his first car,how much I never knew but apparently a princely sum split between the syndicate of three.Saturday, at three o'clock,the games

were all played,all kicked off at the same time and at four forty five,the final whistle blown we gathered around the little bakelite wireless set to await the football results at five o'clock.Armed with the morning paper,which was turned to the list of football fixtures on the back page,pen ready in hand the results were written against each game as the announcer James Alexander Gordon or Timothy Gudgin lilted the results to those of us sat at home.The final results given we could then check them against dad's predictions,twenty four points was the aim,the results scored as three for a draw,one and a half for an away win and one for a home win,extra dividends were paid if there were more than eight draws in total.It also depended if you entered single lines or a full perm.The coupon checked nothing was accepted as being correct until the late results paper with the printed results was obtained.This paper,printed by The Portsmouth Evening News,also gave the number of draws there were on the coupon and how much the dividends amounted to.Before that however we would have tea,most times crumpets or toast toasted on a wire toasting fork over an open coal fire giving it a slightly smoky flavour the bread singed black around the edges,if too singed it would be scraped with a knife,nothing was thrown away,in any case the butter and homemade strawberry jam hid any burnt taste.Wrapped up warm our breath showed like mist in the chill of the full moon and the twinkling stars of the frost laden air.It was only coming up to six thirty,it was going to be a cold night as we walked briskly up the road from the Middlecroft Arms into Cambridge Road where we walked over the level crossing which stood on a slight hump in the road.On the opposite corner to the barbers shop was Molloy's newsagents shop where we joined a little throng gathered outside waiting for the arrival of The Portsmouth Evening News van which had come up from the Gosport ferry with its cargo of blue results 'final''papers.Invariably on the coldest of evenings it was late,late telegraphing of the results holding up the printing,by the time they arrived the throng were stamping their feet,blowing into their hands,tucking them into their armpits.The newspapers unloaded, the men shuffled in as the bundles were cut open,took a paper,handed over the correct money and with a terse"thanks",maybe a comment of"Pompey were unlucky today" they were gone.Paper in hand it was a hurried walk home,where the grown ups rechecked the pools,then read the match reports,me,I just had a hot drink of Horlicks,Ovaltine or Bournville cocoa and retired to a cold bed clutching a red rubber hot water bottle.Goodnight!

****

"Pride comes before a fall"

****

As the summer days became warmer I decided,with a couple of friends to try my hand once more at fishing,although previous attempts had been quite unsuccessful,in spite of efforts from Nana in her endless desire to provide opportunities for me in the difficult time after mum's death.This time I was trusted to go on my own,or at least with one or two trusted friends,so with khaki knapsack containing jam sandwiches and a couple of rock cakes firmly strapped on my back,along with my fishing reel,a tin of lead weights,fishing hooks of differing sizes and "spinners" I bade Nana farewell.A short green fibreglass fishing rod with a cork handle was my choice for the day,the only choice actually as I only had the one,it was a bad choice at that, as it was more of a handicap than a help.It was a long arduous walk,down the length of Whitworth Road,before meeting up with my friends at The White Hart in Stoke Road.Excitedly,we hurried down Stoke Road as we made our way to North Street and Murphy's General Stores,it sold everything,certainly the item I required.Amongst the barbed hooks,nails,brooms,fishing tackle,dustbins,spades and other general hardware was what we had come for.In a wooden box lined with damp newspaper were wriggling,sandy,mud covered listless ragworms,probably dug from the shores of the harbour earlier that morning,the best bait for sea fishing.A few pence worth were placed in a paper bag,so with the wriggling paper bag in our hands we walked down the High Street,past the Gosport Ferry Office a made for the old wooden pier, next to the Portsmouth Chain Ferry which ran across the harbour.Having arrived we sat on the hot surface

of the wooden pier,it had a slight smell of tar which seemed to melt and ooze from it when it was very hot.Under it we could see the ghostly shapes of a shoal of grey mullet almost impossible to catch as their mouths were too soft.Ironically dangling our legs over the side I ate my fish paste sandwiches whilst setting up my fishing gear.With the reels attached to the rods,hooks and weights,in turn attached to the line,the ragworm was threaded onto the hook so I was ready to cast my lines as far as possible.Distance was not our forte,the rods were short,the weights were too light and my arms not quite strong enough,with all the strength I could muster the line sailed out and landed about as far in distance as I could have jumped,the majority of it wrapped around the pontoon I was fishing from.

Some of my friends used "spinners" with more success but the constant casting out and reeling in did not appeal to me and made my arms ache.The little band of us were silently,not very patiently, sat in our shorts our rods laying next to us until a tightening of the line and a dip of the rod tip suggested we had a bite.I fumbled with the rod,struck,to hook the fish,which obviously was of magnificent proportion and began to reel in.It's really pulling it's a big one,wonder what it is went through my excited mind,then breaking the surface of the water was a silver wrasse,weighing at least an ounce,a full two inches in length.Unhooked,the hook was only slightly smaller than the fish,it was returned to the ocean,meanwhile a friend sat next to me who was using a handline,a wooden rectangular frame with the line wound around it,had indeed had a bite from something much larger.As he pulled it to the surface he enlisted our help,it seemed to be heavy but it was the resistance it was providing that made it seem that way,when it appeared on the surface the final pull landed a energetically wriggling eel,about eighteen inches long.Mass hysteria ran along the pontoon as the"conger eel"slithered around and we jumped"like cats on a hot tin roof"trying to avoid it as we had been told"if it bites you it won't let go".Its rapid movement propelled it towards the edge of the jetty,it suddenly shot over the edge dragging the handline with it,my disconsolate friend only left with the tale of "the one that got away"Finally exhausted,mostly after the pandemonium around the eel, we packed up our lines,those of us who still had one and slouched our way home.As we made our way the little group got smaller as individuals split off to go home until I was the last one left.I walked slowly the last few hundred yards,went indoors,deposited my fishing gear in the backyard,someone else could put it away later,usually Nana,and regaled Nana and Grandad with the days fishing tales before wearily falling asleep.

****

"A miss is as good as a mile"

****

As normal as it appeared at the time it now certainly appears to be unusually odd,in fact improbably so.I had known that things would possibly be difficult but what I didn't realise was just how difficult that was to be,nonetheless things that happen are current to the time and not to be judged by modern trends and interpretations.Whenever I walked across the scrubbed doorstep of the old Victorian terraced house I always carried certain things with me,back in those post war years they were seen as normal for then,something which unfortunately cannot always be said for today.Whether I was going to school,the cemetery,shopping or just playing on the pavement I had braved the same barriers come what may.I was expected to take my manners,politeness and respect and most of all my pride in myself and my family,I was equal to anyone we were all here together,I was expected to treat everyone the same,even total strangers were to be accorded the courtesy of politeness.I had been dutifully inspected before leaving home,my hands were clean,there was no dirt under my fingernails,no wax in my ears,no snot running from my nose,and certainly no vestiges of any food anywhere around my person.I had

23

had my hair combed and the parting was straight,I had a clean folded handkerchief,my shoes were polished and laced ,my buttons were all done up,my braces tightly secure,my knees were clean and I was never allowed to eat or drink whilst walking along the pavement,meals were to be eaten at the table and when you left the table you had finished! Fish and chips could be eaten out of the old newspaper it was wrapped in,chewing gum was allowed but you did not spit it onto the pavement,any rubbish went in the bin,streets were spotless and litter laws strongly enforced.As you ventured out there was no shouting,no running,but a leisurely walk,strangers would say 'hello' and you responded,you stood aside and made way for adults,you waited at the kerb to cross the road.You offered help without being prompted,you made way for older folk,you helped them across the road and people pushing prams,especially the big Silver Swan ones,you would help lift off the kerb.In the same way you would help a lady get her pushchair on the bus instead of just watch them struggle and think it funny.You walked around puddles and stepped aside so others didn't have to walk in them,you picked up litter and put it in a nearby bin,you certainly didn't drop any.I remember my sister dropping a cigarette butt and the passing bobby giving her a five pound fine,a fair sum of money in the late fifties.If two adults met and proceeded to chat,I stood quietly,not daring to fidget or whine as it was bad manners and reflected on my upbringing.On the full bus I gave up my seat to older or female passengers,at the shops I never asked for anything to be bought as a treat.What a strange world I grew up in,it was so cruel,the abuse I suffered as a child it was so politically incorrect,my personality was suppressed as well as depressed,I was so unhappy,I had terrible treatment and that was when I was under eleven, before I reached grammar school where physical torture was meted out regularly by gowned teachers wearing mortarboards. If I failed to follow the expected routine it resulted in the administering of the slipper and cane.Do I regret any of it...no,would I have changed it...no did it make me have problems....no.That was just how you were brought up in Gosport,as in most other places in the 1950's......it was the accepted normality of the time and you can't change history or judge by present day ideology.

****

"In for a penny,in for a pound"

****

"Can you call your brother it's dinner time and he needs to wash his hands"I heard Nana say as I sat on the front door step.As I stood up my sister appeared saying"you've got to come in"."I'm coming"I replied,as usual I grumbled about it, but as Nana said"cleanliness was next to godliness",although I had no real perception of what "godliness" was.What the fixation with washing was I have no idea but in times when it needs the world to be told to wash to prevent viral infection there is a lot to learn from the practices of my childhood,perhaps not quite so severe perhaps.We didn't have after shave and deodorants to cover up obnoxious body odours,we had to wash,and not just once a day.Hand washing before meals was the normal practice,even if you had a rare in between meals snack washing hands was still a required action.

  This small almost insignificant action was,however,nothing compared to other habitual requirements.We washed,before going to bed and then on rising in the morning,how dirty a person could get in a clean bed mystified me,but it was expected for you to wash.Having accepted that, we had to also endure a weekly bath which was a bit of a conundrum as it took place on a Friday in a tin bath which hung on the backyard wall all week.An ancient copper which sat in the corner of the scullery was filled with buckets of water and lit as it was gas.The ensuing boiling water was then emptied into the bath using a saucepan then brought to a survivable temperature with saucepans of cold water,There was a hierarchy to bath day,Grandad was first,Nana was last,the rest of us slotted in between,each new bather would have a saucepan of hot water added from the copper,the last person in would be bathing in hot,but dirty water,previously used by everyone else,making the ritual of the bath,to me,rather pointless.Once washed I would endure nothing short of a military inspection to actually get to the pavement the other side of the front door.Having overcome the first hurdle this had similarities to jumping Bechers Brook in the Grand National.

Having arrived at the front door it was like the inquisition,to actually leave to go to school was a mammoth task "let's have a look at your face"was the start,are your shoes polished,are your laces tied,are your garters and tie straight,have you got a clean handkerchief."I hope you put a clean vest and pair of pants on in case you have an accident". The latter not in case I had a toilet incident but in case an accident led me to going to hospital.It continued,"is your parting straight,have you washed behind your ears,is your neck clean,turn your hands over,let's look at your nails"The inside of my shirt collar,my knees,the corners of my mouth,sleepy dust in my eyes.they were all checked and ticked.A brisk walk to school and a further inspection,when lack of a clean handkerchief could mean being sent home.All in all we had hygiene and cleanliness instilled into us,not as a chore simply as part of normal daily life,with it we controlled how often we were ill,without it,as now,we left ourselves open to the likes of poliomyelitis,tuberculosis or worse.

''It's no good crying over spilt milk''

In the nineteen fifties the summers always seemed to consist of blue skies and fluffy white clouds,the days were hot and nights seemed to have been much more humid.The ''pea-soup'' smog with its stinging Sulphur laden clouds would get in the throat and give you a rasping cough.Tuberculosis was still relatively rampant and many people ended up on an uncomfortable,rather primitive,iron lung at an isolation sanatorium.Polio was still a major problem and many people had calipers and built up boots as a way to help them develop the wasted muscles.The winters,however were the exact opposite of those ambient summers,it was freezing cold,the boating lake at Walpole Park froze over and could be skated on the ice was so thick.Frost layed like snow and for many days the frost stayed around all day,never melting it was so cold,icicles hung from trees and the edges of gutters at every house,sometimes falling like daggers onto pavements below.The slippery pavements were cleared of ice with a liberal sprinkling of salt or shovels of coal ash and cinders from the living room fire.Overnight snow lasted for several days,each household would clear the pavements outside their own door,the residents pride not wanting anyone to slip because of them.If they had an elderly neighbour they would clear their path as well.I would build a snowman,every child,and some adults, in the street would have one,a lump of coal for a nose and eyes,twigs for arms they didn't melt for days.The local parks would display a number of enormous snowballs rolled up by groups of children and then just abandoned,the last vestiges remaining long after all the surrounding snow had vanished.Those very cold days,lasting for weeks left the tips of your fingers numb,the cold breath leaving the scarf around your mouth soaking wet,giving rise to a sore red face.These were real winters,we loved them,I remember well the laughter and excitement it generated, never having time to feel cold,we would play all day till you were called in to thaw in front of the welcome open fire.

****

''Treat others,as you would wish to be treated yourself''

****

It was just like many others,a two up,two down Victorian terrace house,red bricks,grey slate roof,soot stained chimney,wooden entrance door with heavy brass door knocker and sash windows.Accommodation inside was a parlour,lounge come dining room,scullery and upstairs two double bedrooms,all serviced by an outside toilet.Bathrooms were unusual unless the house was built after the war,hot running water almost unheard of.This house,however,was no ordinary house, 80 Leesland Road,was the home of Charlie and Annie Brickwood,pensioners who had lived there since the nineteen thirties,now due to tragic circumstances they had found themselves substitute parents to two small children, who had lost their mother and whose father worked endlessly to provide for them,to me they were just my Nana and Grandad.

The memories of the fifties and growing up with them were mixed at times,there were as in any house ups and downs, but the memories I have of these people and the residents of a nothing but ordinary road have stayed with me forever.What I had experienced was underpinned by those innate objects that appeared nondescript but played a major part in everyone's everyday life,For example it was the most basic of things which I remember,they were items which played a large part in life but were mostly overlooked as insignificant.The sash windows with their sash cords and the little brass catch on the middle of the frames that secured them were examples.In the bedrooms,there were the green cast iron brass bedsteads,brass finials standing proudly on each corner of the bed,the"gazunder",so named from its position under the bed,alternatively known as a "jerry",a name associated with the enemy from the recent war,the white and blue enamel candlesticks filled with white Prices candles,purchased by weight and then wrapped in brown paper from Mr Cloggs hardware Shop in Whitworth Road.The windows throughout the house were dressed with mostly unpatterned net curtains,heavy drapes,sometimes ancient blackout curtains,and all were hung on stretched wire or a bamboo rod suspended between two brass cup hooks.The stairs had a carpet runner held in place with highly polished brass stair rods with acorn decorations on their ends,the edges of the stair treads either side of the runner stained and polished.The parlour,the inner sanctum was suitably furnished with the

"best" items and used only on special occasions and Sundays.A small tortoiseshell patterned bamboo table,brown oil cloth settee,two adjustable wooden armchairs,on the floor a handmade rug that had been painstakingly made on those long winter evenings.Over the black ebonised mantel piece,enclosing the black japlaced grate, a square mirror hung above the shelf holding a selection of small japanese satsuma vases.The only other item in the room the front door key lying on the window ledge.

Heavy linoleum covered the floor,it was easy to keep clean,in all of the downstairs living areas,except the parlour where the small rag carpet in front of the fireplace was seen as a luxury,the hallway wall looked as though it had been papered in treacle,a thick brown varnish coating the bottom half of the wall,above the rail,which ran waist high,the walls and ceiling had been distempered white.Once we entered the dining room there was a Victorian cast iron grate,a floral tiled panel on each side,furnished with a small wooden fender,standing on the cardinal red painted hearth was a brass companion set,coal bucket and most importantly hanging from a hook an old wire toasting fork.In the corner,by the back window a bakelite radio stood on a tall side table, its electric power supply provided by a glass battery cell which had to be taken to the local garage to be recharged,something not relished as it was exceptionally heavy.Above the fire, on the mantelpiece, stood a wooden clock,a couple of cheap ornaments,two ebonized elephants with ivory tusks and a jar of coloured spills.The pictures in the room hung on brass picture hooks from a wooden picture rail, every house had a picture of the Queen as a mark of respect and loyalty.The only light was from the gas lamp in the ceiling with its extremely delicate mantle,regularly broken as it was lit by one of the spills from the jar,although it was protected behind a clear glass globe,the gas flow controlled by simple chains,which were pulled up and down.When you entered the kitchen with its lino covered stone floor,scrubbed daily to keep it clean,with carbolic soap,hot water and bristle scrubbing brush.Stood in the corner there was a gas copper,a primitive but trusted vitreous enamel gas stove,that had seen many better days,next to it a white Belfast sink.A bread bin,salt jar,a steel to sharpen knives,a set of scales with iron or brass weights stood on the kitchen table with its well scrubbed pine top.There was,on washdays,a zinc bath,blue bag,a box of Robin starch,a skiffle board,borrowed from Lonnie Donegan,washing dolly,wooden split pegs which had a dual purpose, hanging the washing as well as being used to make children's peg dolls.

Going through the latched back door there was a small wooden meat safe,with a perforated zinc metal door, hanging on the yard wall,this was our only way of keeping fresh food cool.Other items littered the journey,each one with their own special memory ,the hemp coal sacks,the iron cistern and chain,pumice stone,loofahs,carbolic soap,Wrights coal tar soap.TCP,cheese dishes,elm breadboards,meat skewers,butter dishes,jelly moulds,pie funnels,pudding cloths the list is endless but all of them,great parts of the complete jigsaw of growing up.

****

''People in glass houses shouldn't throw stones''

****

''God rest ye merry gentlemen'' or ''Good King Wenceslas'',it was that time of year once more.When passing the open church door at Saint Faiths I could hear the treble voices of choristers singing ''Adeste Fidelis''and ''Hark the Herald Angels''followed by the more sombre''O little town of Bethlehem''.Through the open doorway in the flickering candle light the Nativity scene stood for all to see,a timely reminder as to what Christmas really was all about,not eating,spending money or giving presents but giving thanks to God for the birth of his son Jesus,our saviour, in a lowly stable in Bethlehem.At school we had practiced for ever perfecting the carols for the end of term carol concert and the nativity play,the week before Christmas when the school term had ended the enthusiastic singing spilled out into the streets and Leesland Road was no exception.The congregation and choir from the church would stand at the corner of the little side roads enthusiastically giving their renditions of the popular carols.As they stood in the yellowish glow of the lone gas lamp,swathed in silvery moonlight on the cold crisp evening,their lanterns illuminated the cold ruddy cheeks of the jolly singers.Peering from behind the curtains the residents,not wishing to brave the cold,listened intently as they watched the singers move away to the large house that belonged to Mrs Lucas,where the door opened and a fairly large lady emerged with a tray of mince pies,lemonade and hot mugs of cocoa in return for a stirring rendition of "O come all ye faithful".Carolling over for another year,or was it.Officially it was but armed with the ability,questionable as it was at times,to perform carols,some of the younger members thought that they could supplement their pocket money to pay for presents they hadn't saved for all year."It came to pass" that over the next few evenings partial renditions,sometimes just a single line,accompanied by muttering and giggling would be heard on our doorstep.A knock on the door,an exaggerated,"Ooooooh star of wonder,star of light" and the performance was over.Nana or Grandad would open the door and hand over something edible,a mince pie or sweets and then be wished "Happy Christmas" as it was followed by a couple of pennies.By the end of a week of performances it was rather pleasant to sit in Saint Faiths on Christmas Eve for the carol service,to hear the favourites sung as they were meant to be,before returning home to huddle around the little bakelite valve radio to listen to the carols,sung professionally, from Kings College Cambridge.

****

"Look before you leap"

****

The heavy pale blue pushchair with its white tyred wire spoked wheels turned into Oxford Road propelled by an elderly lady wearing a dark blue overcoat and a matching straw hat held on by a lethal looking weapon in the form of a long steel hat pin.The slightly built lady with grey hair and national health glasses was walking purposefully, the rest of her attire being the sturdy blue low heeled shoes and woollen stockings which covered her legs,under her coat a skirt and full length pinafore.She was not on her own as in the pushchair was me,asleep as usual,but also as usual,I always seemed to stir at the correct moment,that was now,as we passed the houses of people who I had known all my life some in their front gardens who waved as we passed.Mr and Mrs Stubbings who were so kind when mum had died,the Harris's,Collins and our neighbours Mr and Mrs Stevens,the neighbour the other side we only ever knew as "the bachelor".He always rode a bike,wore a light grey coat and was very private and rarely seen except when he went to work and came home.We lived in the last semi detached bungalow at the end of the close,number sixteen,the dark green painted wooden double gates led to a short driveway and pebble dashed garage, which dad had built,the bungalow was directly opposite the entrance to the close.To the right of the drive was a smaller opening leading on to a concrete path around to the back of the bungalow.There was a small rockery to the left of this path,to the right three triangular flower beds,planted patriotically in red white and blue,salvia,alyssum and lobelia grown from seed by dad in his greenhouse,every year the same.Around to the back and we came to the green front door with little panes of glass in the top half,by now I was out of my carriage and running towards the large greenhouse in which I was able to see dad.Sometimes,very rarely, Nana would stay over, but usually she returned to Leesland Road,once I was bathed and in bed,after all she had grandad to look after.

''Do as you would be done by''

Most people in the early 1950's lived very thriftily,''save the pennies'', and my family was no exception,by the mid 1950's many had poorly paid jobs,although there was a great deal of overtime if you were a hard worker and most men were.The state pensions were very basic, and the sayings of the day reflected the need for them to make every penny work for them.''A stitch in time saves nine,Take care of the pennies the pounds will take care of themselves,Make do and mend'' were all such phrases associated with thrift and frugality.Like my family the lingering wartime allotment was still the main source of fresh vegetables,but,some gardens like that of sixteen Oxford Road were also pressed into use.Our allotment,or rather Grandad's allotment was reached through a gate in the fence of the bungalow at number sixteen,a gate opposite the front door dwarfed on one side by a mass of yellow honeysuckle and on the other by a huge purple rhododendron which had a hollow centre,I would delight in hiding in the centre of it having taken the golden retriever with me,after I had ridden him around the garden,yes he was that big,he would hide with me waiting to jump out on Grandad as he shuffled through the gate.Other activities were used to supplement the small income and little crafts and hobbies became a source of earnings.Local growers needed harvest folk and vegetable picking was widely available particularly to women living on their own to help pay the bills.Oxford Road,once you had made you way under the rustic trellis arch covered in sweet scented pink roses,was no exception.In the back garden there was the no longer needed air raid shelter remaining from the war,now used for storage,a huge potato patch and a large lawn.At the very rear was an enormous greenhouse used in the summer months to grow tomatoes and cucumbers which were sold to Mr Sheppard in Whitworth Road.The same greenhouse,heated with a galvanised zinc paraffin heater in winter was used to grow incurve and reflex chrysanthemums in shades of yellow,red,bronze and white which were sold to Guntons the florist in Bemisters Lane.Next to the greenhouse stood a large brick shed,split into two halves one half for storing tools,the other for breeding cage birds,popular at the time and another source of income.Dad would proudly exhibit both the flowers and canaries at little local shows.

****

"Once bitten twice shy"

****

Friday evening and it was time to make sure that everything was ready for the adventure I was to experience for the first time on Saturday morning.In the shed at the bottom of the garden all was a hive of activity,as I timidly pulled the door open,through the crack of the opening I asked dad if I could enter,the last thing I wanted to do was lose one of his prize winning canaries.Inside in large cages,each with a little seed container and a water bottle attached to the wire,some with nesting boxes at the end,were beautiful little birds,their songs incredibly melodic,their variety magical.All of the little birds had rings attached to their legs denoting their identity which had been recorded in written records at the start of their lives.Predominantly a little yellow bird they had markings and bars on their plumage and some had a golden or pinkish colouring on their bodies,most had been born in that very aviary.Dad was checking for health,looking in their bright beady eyes,inspecting the feathers for little red mites, picking only those in the peak of condition for the big day.Most evenings a knock would come on the door from other bird fanciers,either delivering or collecting new birds,or simply coming to discuss the breeding of the much loved breed.Down at Leesland Road a different bird was filling the sky,I would stand on the pavement and watch fascinated as Archie Shepherd,whose wife owned the florists shop opposite to Nanas, arrived every evening on his faithful delivery bike to tend to his avian charges.At the bottom of his garden was a rather ramshackle building made of scrap wood,most pigeon lofts were,he would open this loft to allow his flock of various hued homing,or racing,pigeons,to perform circuits of flight above the roofs.Each circuit the flock would dwindle by one or two until the final few flew into the roost together,succumbing to the temptation of food their exercise over.A very different bird to dads canaries,as they had a dual purpose they would be at the show tomorrow,but only those that weren't taking part in a pigeon racing event.They would be crated in wicker baskets,which were placed in the basket on Archies bike before he rode off to the railway station to send them to exotic places,in the 1950's,like Manchester or Newcastle.Once released from those locations they would amazingly make their way back home where at an estimated time their owner was waiting in expectation to clock them back in.Saturday morning arrived to find us awake very early,before seven o'clock,standing in the aviary placing the tiny birds,once checked into wooden ventilated carrying boxes made of plywood.Once loaded carefully into the car we drove off down Southcroft Road,past Anns Hill cemetery,turned left at the War

Memorial Hospital,then opposite to the White Hart we stopped and entered The Nicholson Memorial Hall.When we entered through the double doored entrance our view was met by a throng of people milling around row upon row of wire fronted bird cages,some occupied but others still awaiting for their incumbents.Dad returned to the car to fetch his exhibits for the day and we located their exhibition homes,each bird entered into their breed classes,there were Borders,Yorkshires,Gloucesters,and various others all set out in groups waiting to be judged.Placed in their cages,fresh sawdust on the base,given food and water, we left the hall to the twittering and singing of many beautiful birds before returning later in the day to find out how we,or rather they,had fared.The morning was long,dinner intervened but at last we returned to see what coloured cards and rosettes,if any, adorned the winning cages,we had won enough classes to be awarded a large silver cup,which stood in our front room for the whole year,standing in the company of others won at various other shows.

****

''Make hay whilst the sun shines''

****

Grandad had wearily walked up Leesland Road having partaken of his lunchtime pint, at The Junction public house near Lees Lane railway crossing gates,as was normal I ran down to the corner of Norman Road where he crossed to the pavement on my side of the road and we walked hand in hand up to number eighty.As we entered I could smell the savoury aroma of the Wednesday stew,beef,lamb or chicken,whatever had started as the Sunday roast,it meant we would have my favourite suet dumplings,instead of potatoes today,we always did on Wednesdays.Hands washed,sat at the little table,grace was recited,dinner then eaten in silence before Grandad retired for his after lunch nap,as normal falling asleep whilst reading the Daily Mirror.More than often with a smouldering roll up cigarette dangling from his lips or clutched between the second and third fingers of his yellow nicotine stained hand.Nana had dressed in her best clothes,put some items in her little grey shopping bag,then checked my cleanliness and tidy appearance,as I was to accompany her,before saying"we're off now Charlie,keep an eye on that fire,don't let it go out,remember you've got to finish that today".Having been woken with a start,clutching at his falling cigarette he replied ''yes I'm just going down to the shed in a minute''.I remember my ears pricking up,Grandad had spent day after day in the shed for several weeks,locking it so nobody could get in,he was banging,sawing endlessly and apart from the odd whiff of cigarette smoke nothing came out."Can I stay with Grandad" I pleaded."No not today we're off to see Uncle Dennis and Auntie Verna,Melvyn might be there'',Nana replied.With that prospect in store it didn't seem to be too bad,Melvyn might take me crabbing in Alver Creek at the back of his house,or possibly out to Stokes Bay where he took me in the spring and early summer bird nesting.At the time,the now rightly illegal hobby ,would see little boys removing eggs"blowing them",then displaying them in a Quality Street tin filled with sand or a shoebox filled with cotton wool.We salved our consciences by ensuring we only removed one egg from the nest,not thinking that if every little boy finding that nest did the same it would soon be totally devoid of all of its eggs.It was only a few more days to Christmas,when we returned home that evening Grandad was once more sat in his chair beside the fire."Did you get it finished"asked Nana."Not quite, it'll need another coat tomorrow then it will be ready".Ready for what I thought,what would be ready.With little hope of knowing,it was certain thatI wasn't going to be told and I was unsure if I would ever be party to this secret that Nana and Grandad so closely shared.

****

"You mustn't take the Lord's name in vain"

****

It was that time of year again,it had all started in the late nineteen fifties,purely by accident,by now it was early sixties and I was able to venture farther on my own.One of my friends at school was a lad named Will who lived in Bury Close,he was the proud owner of a Hornby Dublo electric train set,I say he although I suspect it was his dad Reg who got the most enjoyment from it.Reg was a lovely man,who would ride his heavy black Raleigh bicycle in a very upright manner,to and from his work in Fleetlands every day, come rain or shine,his wife,whose name I can't recall was the catalyst of my friendship.When I went around to number seven to play,I was always made welcome and I was always asked to stay for a delicious tea.When I visited,walking up the drive through green painted wooden gates,the anticipation of the exciting prospect of playing with that fantastic railway layout knew no bounds.Climbing the ladder into the loft,the light in the attic illuminated the most awe inspiring train set ever,it covered the whole of the area.The locomotives emitted smoke from their funnels,the lights in the pullman carriages lit up,level crossing gates,the turntable in the locomotive shed all functioned,trains hurtled through the stations controlled by the electrically operated points and signals.It was like being in heaven,I spent many a happy day there when it was too wet to play outside.The reason for today's visit however was early in the morning and I was dressed in a raincoat and sou'wester when I arrived to meet Will.He was similarly dressed when he joined me and we made our way to the White Hart in Stoke Road,opposite the Methodist church which Will's family worshipped at.As we hurried along between the showers,the wind,a brisk one,blew the rain into our faces,everything was set strangely enough for a fine day.Where we were heading this was just the weather we needed,possibly the wind a bit stronger than needed.We walked past the Forum,then Nobes,Greens Cake Shop,Churchers,eventually at Spring Garden Lane we turned into Walpole Park and walked in the direction of Alver Creek.Before reaching the creek we cut across behind the outdoor swimming baths to our destination,the boating lake.This was the lake that had witnessed the demise of my battery powered Airfix landing craft as it sunk in the middle,today was hopefully going to be less traumatic,more exhilarating.As we breasted the bank and looked down to the lake we spotted what we had come for,the gathering in front of us was one of superb wooden pond yachts,their attentive owners from far and wide,the only missing piece was the crews that they needed to sail them,which was where we came in,we were hoping to provide some of those crews.We made our way down to the edge of the pond waiting for the invite,knowing if we accepted, one of the international skippers would reward us well at the end of the week.In no time a man smoking a strange smelling cigarette from France approached us and in broken English and hand movements asked if we would like to crew for him and his compatriot,to which we willingly agreed.Crewing comprised of helping to lift the impressive large wooden yachts in and out of the water at which time the skipper trimmed the sail,decided whether to use a spinnaker or not and at the starting gun gently pushed the boat on its way.The wind direction blowing off the creek was certainly unpredictable and as we walked armed with a wooden pole down either side of the lake our services were frequently required to stop the boat hitting the side,before setting it once more on its course.Winning was very exciting,if you did well you would be invited to return the following day and to crew for the remainder of the week.Week over,goodbyes said,you would leave with a reward of as much as five pound from a successful owner but more normally half a crown or five bob.Will you be back next time they would ask,two years was a long time,the following year they would be racing in Southport so who knows what we would be doing when they returned.

****

''Let sleeping dogs lie''

****

Back to school and how different it was,first day back and we had to be properly''turned out''.To give me plenty of time to get ready I was woken up very early,well seven o'clock,to me,was early.A hearty breakfast of a boiled egg and soldiers, it was time to have a good wash.''Don't forget to use the flannel'',''I won't''I shouted back.Having washed,now it was time to get dressed.my clothes were laid on a nearby chair,long grey socks with elastic garters,pants string vest.short sleeve shirt,short sleeved jumper and the dreaded tie.Once dressed I ran down stairs and donned a pair of black lace up shoes before combing my hair, so I didn't get ''nits''I was told.I was then ready for inspection.having passed muster I was allowed to go,when I left I was in perfect condition but it was when I had arrived at the school gates that I presented a very different picture.I had fallen over and scraped my knees,my hankie was blood stained and my hair all over the place.My shoes were scuffed,my tie twisted round the back of my neck,my trousers had a tear in them and my face was dirty as I had not wiped all the egg off of it in the very corner of my mouth,which Nana for once had missed.To cap it all today we were to be inspected by''the nit nurse''on her regular visit.Oh well we could always have another try tomorrow,practice makes perfect and each day was another chance to get right,you see it was to do with pride and example.Nana's pride and my example.

****

''Make do and mend''

****

The Thursday before Christmas, Grandad once more after dinner had made his way, having had his siesta,to the garden shed.I tried very hard as he entered to see what was in their as he gently pushed me way,through the narrow gap all I could see in the gloom was a white sheet that was covering something I was obviously not meant to see.I returned indoors and knelt on the armchair,the radio playing Mrs Dales Diary,which was broadcast at a quarter to three everyday,followed by Woman's Hour.Watching through the raindrops running down the window pane,waiting impatiently for Grandad's return from the shed,hoping he would bring something out providing me with a small clue as to what was taking place inside.There was to be no such luck,or was there.Entering the scullery I ran out to be greeted by the smell of what I now know was turpentine and Grandad was washing his hands in the belfast sink,trying to remove what looked to me like grey and red paint.But if it was paint,what had he been painting,what was so important that I mustn't see it.My imagination was in top gear,not even knowing if it was something for me,as nothing was said,the shed remained locked,the days went by,but still nothing.Perhaps the excitement of the build up to Christmas must have diverted my attention at some time but on the Monday,two days before the big day,when the mangle was taken out to wring water from the weekly washing there was nothing in there.Someone had either smuggled something out when I wasn't looking or what had been taking place in there the week before was partially my imagination and to be of no consequence to me.All the tools were in their rightful place,nothing was missing,there was a sprinkling of sawdust on the floor,maybe a rag in a different place but nothing that wasn't there the last time I had been in the shed."What was Grandad doing in the shed"I asked Nana,"just tidying things up and doing some repairs "she replied,and I just shrugged my shoulders and went back in to play.Two more days passed and Christmas morning arrived,I was up early,down the stairs and excitedly entered the dining room.My stocking was taken down and I delved in it to find the orange,banana,apple and assorted nuts.Small neatly wrapped gifts,wax crayons,pencils,a notepad a bar of chocolate,Christmas had been good to me,I was happy with what I had received.The stocking empty I was given a present which I was told I mustn't open till after breakfast so although too excited to eat much I sat obediently at the table till we had all eaten."Can I open it now" I asked,"Go on then" said Nana,impatiently I began to tear off the festive paper only to be reminded to open it properly so that the paper could be reused the following year.Eventually the removal of the paper revealed a box of painted wooden toy soldiers something I had always wanted,better still however was to come."If you go into the front room there is something else",said Nana.I needed no further invitation,running up the hallway,flinging open the front room door there in front of me was a large homemade wooden fort.At last I had found out Grandads secret and I was so happy he had let me share it at last.

****

''He who laughs last laughs loudest''

****

It was a gloomy day with rain falling like stair rods, bouncing off the paving stones and granite road chippings as it fell,there were no puddles,no potholes,there wasn't enough traffic on the roads to generate them,apart from that the vehicles didn't carry very heavy loads.Besides that,the fact was that the maroon Gosport Borough Council, Aveling and Porter,steam road roller did its job so well the surface was smooth and even,everyone taking pride in the results of the job they had undertaken.The granite kerb stones made sure the rainwater stayed in the gutters,no litter blocking the rivulets as the water sped towards the heavy cast iron gratings and on into the drains.The road sweeper with his electric handcart,stiff bristled broom and large shovel made sure no obstructions stood in its way ensuring everything flowed freely on his daily rounds.The caped midwife,her cape flowing behind her,pedalled furiously through the rain, a new baby,maybe a brother or sister for somebody, needed her company on it's entry in to this world and Nurse Skinner was the lady to give it.Further along the road the red gold-lettered electric Co-op bread van purred along the road,the little red Commer van,similarly signed delivered its Co-op groceries from the little store which stood opposite Central School.Its regular driver,who had been delivering since the war, would knock on the unlatched doors,enter,then place the weeks groceries on the little wooden dining table,trust was implicit.The baker likewise,carrying his wicker bread basket filled with all manner of crusty loaves did the same,if you were home he would offer you a cheap stale loaf with which to make bread pudding.Mr Stanley,the log merchant would deliver logs in a wicker basket,taking them through the house to the backyard where he would stack them by the coal shed.Mr Shepherd delivered fruit and vegetables,seasonal of course,no imported items to extend the season. Mr Blundell the coalman carried his hundredweight sacks of coal,my job being to count them in,over a white dust sheet covering the polished floor, careful to avoid any damage to the thick heavy linoleum with his heavy boots.On the pavements the pedestrians with their macs and umbrellas still found time to utter a greeting as they hurried along,daily life continued bad weather or not,as did courtesy and manners.The gas lamp lighter still paused for his cigarette under the lamp,rain dripping off his oilskins as he stood opposite the junction of Norman Road,the local ginger tom still hunted on the empty bomb site a little further down near number sixty.As the gloom turned to dusk the rain still beat down,as the almost uniformly attired cyclists,keen to get home to the dry, beat their way home from the days toil at Ashleys wallpaper factory in Lees Lane by the railway crossing,their numbers swelled by workers from the naval armament supply depots at nearby Priddy's Hard,Bedenham,Frater,the aircraft repair yard at Fleetlands or from the biggest employer in the area H M Royal Naval Dockyard in nearby Portsmouth. As the curtains closed,so did the doors,the wet pavements now echoed with the sound of silence,Leesland Road returned to it's solitude of night time,dimly lit it's quietness rarely broken after darkness had fallen,an almost self imposed curfew,reminiscent of the wartime blackout,but now this was the year 1955.

****

"Don't let the cat out of the bag"

****

In the 1950's we walked along what was just a muddy path full of puddles,Mile Lane,one side of it was bordered by the fences of the bungalows in Southcroft Road,the other a weed grown hawthorn hedge which was the boundary of Anns Hill cemetery,before it became allotments when the cemetery came to an end.It ran all the way to the Military Road although there was a cut through which came out opposite Oxford Road and as we reached the end of the allotments an even muddier path which led to Privet Park.I would use it when going with Nana from Leesland Road to where we lived in Oxford Road,it was more interesting than walking up Southcroft Road and its cloned pebble dashed bungalows.At the top of Southcroft Road lived my music teacher as for some reason it was felt that I should learn to play the piano,such an instrument we had at home,a legacy of mum.My music teacher who was a bit of a tyrant was Mrs Diaper,a short,slightly stout,black haired lady who delighted in rapping my knuckles with a ruler if I was presumptuous enough to play a wrong note,you must practice more she would say,Saturday mornings were much to be looked forward to.It was as I was going with my dad and sister in that direction for my sisters lesson that we witnessed a tragedy at first hand.It was apparent that when the sound from a passing helicopter suddenly changed that there was about to be an impending disaster.Within moments from behind the bungalows in the vicinity of the allotments a pall of black smoke rose into the sky witnessing the final resting place of the Royal Navy helicopter as it crashed resulting in the death of its pilot.As other residents came out to see the cause of the commotion we turned and headed back home,no lessons that day and a February day in 1954 not to be forgotten.

''Don't count your chickens before they hatch''

Opportunities in my later years have enabled me to remember things that erstwhile I had forgotten and the coronavirus covid19 pandemic afforded me such an opportunity with a good deal of time on my hands.What should I do to spend the generous time offered me by fate, it was not to be wasted,so I decided to make an excursion into the past,to the time when I was a small boy,it seemed too good to miss out on.An excursion into an everyday tale was shortened by fate but it left me wondering what to do.I was a key worker so still covered my shifts, albeit from home and so idly I started to think about the jobs that had been performed long before automation when I was a little lad,the blacksmith,pigman,carter,trout tickler cobbler and many more.What an opportunity I thought to do a family tree for the grandchildren.So it began and as with most families my ancestors much the same as most peoples,there were labourers,sailors,general dogsbodies and many of them spent a substantial amount of time as paupers in the Alverstoke workhouse.However suddenly I realised that my position in life was again destined by fate as suddenly Elizabeth of York and Henry VIII appeared as ancestors,indeed my uncle William le ber,married to Auntie Flo was a direct descendant,not a blood relative to me but close enough.Checked and double checked I couldn't believe that a Gosport old boy had been deprived of his opportunity of greatness.Excitedly I told my five year old grandson who now thinks the Queen is my mum and we are going to live in Buckingham Palace when she dies.Think we may have a problem but will save it and return to that family tree when they are a little older.Stay safe and give it a go yourself.....after all somebody must have God as an ancestor.

The fact is that in a family tree we can go back years but we really know very little of the people on it,unless they were famous.This in the present time leads us to knowing so little about the parents grandparents,cousins and other relatives we have lived with,we have moved now from a culture of not speaking to those people,to one where we need to ask those very people about their lives.The era after the war was one where people had been trained not to gossip,"Idle words costs lives",this had such an impact that people were exceptionally private and it remained the culture for many years.So many memories have been lost because of that,tomorrow will be too late,for many already that is the case,it must be done today before it is lost forever and another generation will say."I wish I had asked so many things when they were alive.

****

Don't put all your eggs in one basket"

****

The diminutive figure was dressed in flannel pyjamas and a blue and grey tartan squared dressing gown secured by a shiny satin cord around his waist,its silky tasselled ends reaching down to his knees.The pocket had a white handkerchief spilling from it,on his feet rubber soled,woollen cloth slippers kept his toes warm and in one hand a mug of hot chocolate, in the other a pink wafer biscuit.That morning when he had come down the stairs the normal smell of the porridge at breakfast time was not so strong as normal,it was almost overcome by the uncommonly savoury steam which was temptingly drifting from the kitchen.Work in the kitchen had started early that morning,there was a great deal to do and by early evening people would be arriving at the door and they would be in a hurry and couldn't wait.The smells had continued all day,temptingly delicious and deliciously diverse,in some instances it was the ingredients themselves that provided part of the magic,parsley,fresh from the garden left a fragrant scent as it was pushed through the mincer,the green juice dripping onto the enamel plate placed to catch it as it fell.Bread being dried in the oven to make breadcrumbs had a warm toasted aroma,the raw onions following the already minced parsley in the mincer induced a tear or two as the cook turned the mincer handle.On the little gas stove the largest aluminium pot I had seen emitted steam reminiscent of a Wednesday stew,as the oven door opened the smell of sausage meat wrapped in shortcrust pastry drifted out.As the day progressed the smells changed,fruity mincemeat in shallow pastry cases replaced the sausage rolls,warm cheese straws and warm strawberry milk jelly and milky chocolate blancmange.The kaleidoscope of smells was non stop but they added up to only one thing,it was Christmas Eve.Tomorrow was Christmas Day and if everything wasn't prepared for the following day in time,the smooth success of the Christmas meal would be nothing short of a disaster.

****

''Don't beat about the bush''

****

Now time had run out,if it hadn't been done it was too late.By the early evening the warm glow from the lonely gas lamps lit a street which was becoming deserted,there was a chill in the air,every time the front door opened the cold air crept in,it really felt like Christmas had arrived at last.Outside in the same street people were scurrying home,many laden with heavy bags,shops were now closed,the only sounds bicycle bells and people shouting"Merry Christmas" as their paths crossed in the street.The Christmas fare,Nanas Christmas present to the family had been distributed as Uncle Dennis,Uncle Bert,and Dad arrived and collected a stuffed fresh chicken,complete with neck and giblets wrapped separately,homemade Christmas plum pudding,a dozen mince pies dusted with icing sugar,traditionally a baker's dozen of thirteen,and a similar quantity of sausage rolls.Whilst Nana was fetching it all,putting it all in bags, a glass of sherry,dry or cream,ginger wine and a mince pie or homemade peppermint cream or marzipan fruit would be enjoyed.

But now they had all gone,I was curled up on the little woollen rag rug in front of a flickering coal fire,next to me huddled up was an exhausted Nana,puffing away in a fireside chair sat Grandad,enjoying a Winston Churchill cigar,after all it was Christmas.In the background the little bakelite valve radio quietly played popular seasonal carols sung by a church choir,occasionally we would join in,most were known off by heart.The light from the gas lamp on the ceiling had been replaced by that of two dancing white wax candles,the light reflecting off the foil and glitter decorating some of the cards,the paper chains and chinese lanterns dancing in the rising heat.Empty stockings hung by the fireside,it was time for bed,I was certainly ready,my eyes were heavy and I was fighting to stay awake.Picking up a candlestick "to light me to bed"I kissed Grandad on his stubbly cheek and stumbled up to bed,Nana's steadying hand on my shoulder prevented me from falling,who knew what tomorrow would bring.

****

"It's raining cats and dogs,coming down like stair rods"

****

"Diddle,diddle dumpling my son John".what did it mean was it just a street sellers catchphrase,as an infant we grew up on such silly nursery rhymes.They were seen as innocent,maybe slightly naive meaningless jingles,children laughed and giggled innocently,repeated parrot fashion what were just stupid words,there meanings not really understood ."Hear we go gathering nuts in May"was sung as groups of children danced in and out around the maypole,we never thought that nuts and frosty mornings were autumn features,but did it matter.As with so many of our childhood rhymes the words had been corrupted over the years,the real words"knots of may",simply a bunch of hawthorn flowers.I remember reciting "Baa baa black sheep have you any wool"nothing underlying this simple rhyme,just the sharing of fleeces to clothe the various residents.However some were surprisingly violent,"Humpty Dumpty","The Grand Old Duke of York",others amusing "Four and twenty blackbirds".Some seemingly funny rhymes had more unsavoury undertones and were not all the first appeared."Georgy,Porgy pudding and pie"a reference to the gluttony and bawdy behaviour of a previous monarch."Ring a ring a roses" an apparent pleasant childish game in fact a direct reference to the plague of medieval times.The one however I remember innocently laughing at was "Jack and Jill went up the hill to fetch a pail of water"a daily chore which was not unusual,fortunately the rhyme was not too descriptive as to what the two of them got up to at the top of the hill.Needless to say that whatever it was,I will leave to your imagination,but resulted in the unfortunate demise of both parties.These little rhymes were constantly employed to amuse the infant,me,however like many other things their popularity has waned and these simple traditions are beginning to disappear.

"Time flies when you are having fun"

April had arrived accompanied with its predictable showers,sometimes these could be heavy showers with thundery overtones,most as soon as they arrived however,had passed uneventfully.May was a better prospect arriving with a warning which it was best to heed,"don't cast a clout till May is out"the showers, less frequent,were replaced by cool breezes which as the month progressed became warmer heralding a more summery period to follow.Whether the rhyme referred to the month of May or the white,sometimes red, flowers of the hawthorn or may tree is open to some conjecture.Today was a typical May day,not too hot yet not too cold,as I lay on the short grass surrounded by buttercups and young children making daisy chains,the maypole on the green was ready to be forgotten for another year.The sky above was clear and vividly blue,not a cloud to be seen,just the singing of a lone skylark climbing forever upwards before plummeting to earth to a hidden nest in the tussocks of grass.It was then that the steady distinctive drone of a Merlin engine interrupted my dream announcing the arrival of a lonely Spitfire,reminiscent to many of an era gone by, ascending from the grass airfield at nearby Grange. The pulsating throb increased as it climbed its way towards the horizon,it was at peace with the world at last, after years of conflict, as it vanished from sight the day soon returned to its lazy quietude just the birdsong remaining.

Laying there it was the more natural sounds that excited me,those of the soaring skylark,that of a blackbird in the nearby holly tree,which occasionally ascended to a raucous alarm call,warning of the impending approach of a marauding "moggy".The constant underlying hum of a solitary bumble bee as it zig zagged across the blades of grass in search of a hole in the grass in which to lay its egg.Sulphur coloured Brimstone and Orange Tip butterflies searched out stinging nettles to lay their eggs on,a favoured food for their ravenous caterpillars,sometimes they were joined by a Large White or Holly Blue variety.Hoverflies hung above the yellow dandelions,their tiny wings beating Incessantly,holding them in position above the flowers,sending little fluffy seeds drifting across the flower beds.On the red brick path black or red ants scurried busily around as they crossed the silvery trails left by the previous nights visiting slugs or snails.A pile of empty snail shells signalled the presence of a song thrush that had had a good breakfast,or was it a hungry brown rat.The idyll was suddenly broken,once more, not by the returning Spitfire but by the warning bell of a responding emergency ambulance in the distance,it was too hot and too far away for us to investigate its route.In the neat weed free garden borders edging the new mown lawn, the display of spring bulbs,apart from a lingering tulip,were all but finished,having been supplanted by the reddish brown and yellow of the wallflowers and polyanthus,bought the previous autumn from the greengrocers,neatly wrapped in wet newspaper.A purple mauve rhododendron,the commonest shade,was bursting into the football size blooms which made it so stunning,the fashionable rockery,made of old paving and salvaged stone,sported purple aubrieta,white arabis and yellow stonecrop tumbling from the nooks and crannies running between its recycled hardware.Garden spades rang as they met with flint or stone hidden under the fertile earth,hoes glided through the vegetable rows beheading any alien infiltrators,the click click of the hedging shears trimmed the bushes and hedges into shape.What an idyllic solitude this proved to be.I opened my eyes as a voice said "would you like a drink" I realised then how time had changed.It had taken sixty five years and an insidious virus,similar to poliomyelitis in my youth to return me once again to that far flung almost forgotten time.Yes the events of now had returned me to those much missed memories of sixty years before.

****

''You're guess is as good as mine''

****

Nineteen forty nine was a remarkable year,apart from the fact that it was the year I was born,it was,unwittingly at the time for me,the start of memories that I have retained from the mid 1950's,when life was less complicated and demanding,the time before technology took over it was the year that the viral epidemic,poliomyelitis, started which was to similarly to the covid19 pandemic affect so many people,bringing much anguish and misery to what was then many people.The older people could remember the Spanish flu epidemic in 1919 and had lived with tuberculosis for most of their lives.now it is largely forgotten.At the time it affected much of the population of the British Isles,including that of Gosport.I had always wondered,but in those times it was impolite to ask,why my gran from Ireland wore iron calipers and similarly why Mr Clogg in Leesland Road wore an enormous heavy black boot and walked with a stick.I remember being chastised on more than one occasion for eating blackberries that I had picked from the hedgerow without first washing them,similarly I was constantly told not to play around or go near to areas where there were pools of stagnant water as it was felt these were also sources of polio.On one occasion I recall a cream coloured ambulance which I saw arrive to pick up a young lad,he seemed in good health except for a persistent cough and shortness of breath.He was the victim of tuberculosis,a prevalent disease,which was on the wane at this time due to a new vaccine,but for too many this would be a few years too late.Put into isolation,often far from home, some recovered but weakened for ever,others were not so lucky and never returned home.Now it was the turn of this long known virus,polio, to reach epidemic proportions before it too succumbed to a vaccine.The fact was that it was spread from person to person,the initial symptoms involving fever and respiratory problems,the outcome resulting in possible death or physical disabilities,hence those calipers and built up boots.Isolation was a lonely existence as children,like myself,were separated from their parents for many weeks,their ventilator being the "iron lung",a fairly primitive aid to breathing.At the time the fear gripping our parents must have been similar to that,as parents sixty years later,are now experiencing,with no effective cure yet in sight.By May 5th 1956 over half a million children had been vaccinated in the United Kingdom,that protection is still now afforded to us from birth.In the fifties poliomyelitis mostly infected children,that same age group,who are now in their seventies,are now most vulnerable to coronavirus.Hopefully a vaccine isn't far away and covid19 will be a treatable thing of the past, but it just emphasises the fact that probably even though polio is an almost forgotten illness,unless you were scarred by it,it is just a skeleton in a cupboard to many people.A timely reminder that we should take the free time we have had thrust on us,a time when families should be talking more to tell this following generation that will replace us, what it was like in our "dinosaur" years.

****

"Too many cooks spoil the broth"

Dad was in a football pools syndicate in the 1940/50's with Archie and Lofty Shepherd,two brothers who lived in the Whitworth Road area of osport..Archie used to deliver fruit and vegetables using a horse and cart,which was stabled in Smith Street,further down Whitworth Road,close to the piggeries.When Christmas arrived he would take on an additional duty,he would come in my Nanas and dispatch the chickens which had been reared for christmas dinner.Painful duty complete he would take his"blood money" and partake of a proffered "christmas drink" before he left.Lofty,his brother, had a big green high sided furniture pantechnicon,used for house moving,which was also kept in the yard at the piggeries in Smith Street. I knew both of them as always gruffly kind men,always ready with a friendly word when I was about eight! Smith Street was a short cul de sac,half way down Whitworth Road,running down to the piggeries where Alan Barnes tended to his porcine charges.Shepherds yard was an almost rural farmyard in the midst of a residential area indeed it was only one of several dotted around the town,it had a market garden with glasshouses behind it which grew tomatoes cucumbers and flowers.I used to cut through the street to the back of Vernon Close on my way to and from school up until I left primary school in 1961,on the corner of the little street stood a shop which I seem to remember was a small grocers.Virtually every corner had a shop on it,many times they were simply the front room of a little two up two down end of terrace house.I remember on the corners of the streets off of Whitworth Road,a cycle shop,vegetable shop,butchers,grocers,sweet shop,wool shop and Co-op,and this was only on the corners as other shops had sprung up in the terrace houses in between.The few corners not occupied by shops were populated by public houses,The Gypsy Queen and The

Junction being most popular.

"Give them enough rope and they'll hang themselves"

My small step,as I wasn't very old,over the threshold across the doorstep onto the pavement was greeted,not by the army of little black workers which was normally there, building up little piles of silver sand grains around the cracks in the paving stones,but a host of large silver winged flying insects emerging from the same holes that had been excavated by the ants.Some of the scuttling throng had already started to fly and it was necessary to brush them away as they launched themselves blindly into the air,flying into my face,entangling themselves in my hair and landing on my shirt."Nana",I yelled "there's horrible flying things out here quick".A grey wise head dutifully emerged from the open door,"there flying ants,I'll get a kettle of boiling water"she said,"you run down the shop,I'll get rid of them before you get back,off you go".As bid I dodged the aerial bombardment,flapping my arms to brush them away and ran down Leesland Road to number 66a,the little corner shop at the junction of Norman Road.The small shop was in fact the converted front room of an end of terrace house,like so many,but in that tiny space was a well stocked grocery shop with all the things you might need,items you had forgotten to buy when doing the weekly shopping .The deliveries to this little emporium were made through large, brown painted, wooden, double gates which entered on to the backyard of the property from Norman Road.On the red brick wall of the shop,next to the yard,there were three large enamel signs in bright colours,dark blue,orange and yellow,starting to rust in places where the enamel had begun to chip away,having been

57

impacted by the odd stick or stone thrown by a mischievous school child.They advertised Lyons Tea,Brooke Bond Dividend Tea and Colman's Mustard,accompanying the street nameplate high on the wall.The door to enter the cramped shop was on the corner of Leesland Road and like the gates painted brown,it consisted of a solid wooden bottom half with two vertical panes of glass in the top half,split by a further strip of painted wood.A reversible open and closed sign hung on a cup hook,clearly visible through the glass from outside,it was occasionally accompanied by a roughly scrawled paper bag declaring''back in five minutes',as you stepped over the little step into the shadowy interior you were greeted by a jolly man and his equally jolly   .

The floor,or what you were able to see of it,due to the amount of stock that stood on it,was well worn wood,worn down through years of countless feet trampling to the counter in order to be served.There was little room due to the counters being both to the left and rear of the well stocked shop,meaning that as few as three people would constitute a crowd.

On the left,were shelves all around the shop behind the counter,to the right behind the door there were more laden shelves under which was stacked a wooden barrel which dispensed vinegar and wooden crates of various loose items.Following on from the end of these shelves was the passage to the rear of the premises where the living accomodation was situated along with a tiny scullery.In the little passageway standing,on a small table,was a white Avery cooked meat machine next to a red Berkel bacon slicer,its spinning blade hand driven by a large handle.Returning to the shop,on the narrow counter at the rear was a wicker basket displaying loaves of uncut crusty bread,next to which was a long,shallow wooden tray,lined with greaseproof paper. In the tray was a cake selection,including some containing fresh cream, there was no chill chain or refrigeration,other than a small ice cream chest freezer which stood in the corner,you relied on it not getting too warm.Whatever it was that you needed Mr Horne and his wife would have it and if they didn't they would obtain it for the next time you visited.Mr Horne loved children coming in and in a time when sweets were short due to sugar rationing he always managed to produce one from a bag under the counter much to the delight of the receiving child.I can remember him as a slightly flushed faced jolly man,always smiling,with a twinkle in his eye,he had a small white moustache and greying,brush backed,hair with black rimmed spectacles.He always dressed very smartly in grey trousers,an off white linen jacket and the all important bow tie.His wife was slightly shorter,neither were very tall and she also wore glasses,she always appeared as a fussing,loyal wife,grey hair neatly permed,normally dressed in a floral pinafore smock.I remember that due to the size of the shop and the area behind the counter being restricted,it was necessary for her to pass items to her husband as he was slightly portly and passing each other proved to be a bit of a problem at times.They were always in accord,happy to chat,their small shop was the focal point of the local community,the hub of the local residents' daily lives.I think during any given day all the residents of that part of Leesland Road would have paid at least one daily visit to catch up with local news.

****

''Don't put off till tomorrow what can be done today''

****

As I walked past Dad's grocers shop I noticed something different in the window,or rather the door,right in the middle was a large colourful poster advertising Billy Smarts circus which was on its way to

59

Gosport.The times and days were clearly advertised along with the venue,the entrance price in those days only at the reach of a few more wealthy individuals.Unless sacrifices were being made for you to be treated,a treat in those times only came once a year unless it was free,then the only other chance was a complimentary entrance.By the time I arrived at Nana's later that afternoon I had thought a good deal about the poster and excitedly told her there was a circus coming to town."When is that"she asked,"perhaps your dad will take you".Perhaps,I thought but doubted it as he was always too busy,having two jobs was fine,it meant we lived comfortably,but I rarely saw him.Occasionally over the next few days I thought about that poster but it wasn't until the next week that it came to the forefront once more.I don't recall the day of the week but I was with Nana on my way back from Alverstoke when my attention was drawn to an excess of noise coming from close to the White Hart public house at the top of Stoke Road.As we got closer the noise became louder and soon we saw that a little crowd,which people were rushing to join,was starting to fill the pavement.Walking along the road a tall man, resplendent in red coat,black top hat and carrying a very long whip was leading what appeared to be a procession.Slowly walking,the sound of trumpets and drums getting ever closer was a sight I had never beheld before.I had seen animals before,I had seen large animals before,cattle sheep and pigs,they were a common sight in all the local fields and countryside.I had glimpsed mice,foxes,even the odd weasel,but coming down along Bury Road was a column of animals I had only seen till now in nature books.A few paces behind the man came colourfully dressed funny clowns,throwing sweets for children as they went,performing the odd somersault or cartwheel,pretending to throw buckets of water at the crowd now standing at the roadside.In the nearby shops I noticed more of the posters I had seen in Dad's shop, they were everywhere and this was why,"the circus had come to town".At this point,the clowns playfully ran in and out of the crowd and it was at this point my jaw dropped,walking along the road each led by a man carrying a stick,were enormous elephants,trunks waving,ears listening,each with an iron chain around one of its legs.They lumbered slowly down the road,looking incredibly bored,their tiny eyes straining to see,on some sat a pretty lady dressed in silk,satin and sequins,the circus parade was in full swing.They had arrived earlier at the railway station and had walked on a tour of Gosport before they eventually arrived at their quarters in Walpole Park,waving their trunks,their tiny twinkling eyes seeming out of place in such a large animal.Moving along other exotic animals appeared,camels,lions,tigers,then horses,ridden by cowboys and indians whooping and firing cap guns to add to the noise.Acrobats and trapeze artists dressed in shiny costumes waved majestically as they walked passed smiling.By the time the entourage arrived at the park they all must have been exhausted but by the following evening they would be ready to give a performance.The spectacle was like a mobile zoo and in many cases as near to these animals that many children would ever get.With reflection it was definitely a thing of the day when the poor animals were to be gawped at with their welfare and feelings a long way down the list of priorities,it was just another way to earn a living.

****

''One swallow doesn't make a summer''

****

I turned the corner into the narrow road of terraced houses,there was very little traffic,a few cars were parked at the side of the road,the only sound the hum of a random petrol engine as someone made their way Home from their sales representatives job.Unsurprisingly bicycles and pedestrians were more numerous than expensive motor vehicles which the vast majority of people did not have enough money to buy.The little corner shop,Hornes,standing on the corner of Norman Road had a steady trickle of customers as was normal,last minute purchases before they closed at five o'clock,no late night shopping,if you didn't have an item by then you will have to wait till the morning.The alternative was to knock on the neighbours door and ask if you could borrow it,the neighbour content with the thought that it would always be repaid.Shops had half days on Wednesdays and Saturdays,opened nine till five on the other week days,never opened Sunday,God's day of rest and always closed one hour at midday for lunch.Even factories closed one hour for lunch for the workers to eat their packs of homemade sandwiches,the slices of bread the thickness of doorsteps.Everyone knew the hours,made their purchases within those hours and managed their time accordingly.As the streets quickly emptied,evening was beginning to fall,there was a strange quietness as doors closed and residents settled in for the night.In winter it was like a ghost town,in summer everybody would be in their gardens or maybe go for a ''stroll''.Passers-by,even those who were strangers to us,where acknowledged with a poignant "goodnight",it was the polite thing to do.Children were having a last play before bedtime,some listening to a story from a treasured book,passed down from generation to generation,I remember ''The Water Babies'' by Charles Kingsley.In the summer the tiny back gardens echoed with chattering voices,the adults talking over the garden walls and fences exchanging gossip,puffing on a cigarette or briar and catching up with the day's events.No aircraft soared overhead with distant destinations in their sights,no white vapour trails,just blue cloudless skies and chirping crickets,twittering birds and the hum of honey bees.The chink of garden tools,the whirr of hand propelled lawn mowers,immaculate lawns,symetrically planted flower beds and the fresh smell of rain on warm earth.The banging,tapping,sawing,chiselling and chopping from the garden sheds betrayed that repairs were in progress,improvements being made or simply broken items renewed.Make do and mend,it was cheaper to extend the life of something than to buy new,more often than not the money wasn't available in any case.The old rusty screws were re-used,pieces of wood adapted to effect a temporary,or if possible a permanent repair.In the kitchens the smell of baking cakes wafted from windows and back doors,it was cheaper than buying them,all housewives could cook,nothing fancy,simple rock buns,fairy cakes,jam tarts or Victoria sponge,the older women probably having spent a proportion of their early lives "in service".Indoors,in winter time, as it became too dark to stay out,board games and charades were fashionable,stories were told and books were read,grandad would sit with his paper and bottle of stout,Nana would be repairing

clothes,sewing,darning and patching all but the irretrievable,giving them a new lease of life. Bread and butter,with homemade jam,homemade scone or a sponge cake was mostly what tea consisted of,simple food was the best,more than often the only food.Water was the readily available drink,squash and fizzy drinks a luxury and were available only as treats.People talked to each other uninterrupted,as children "didn't speak unless spoken to",and certainly not at the table.There was natural life all around mustard and cress,on sodden blotting paper was grown in a saucer on the window sill,fresh picked flowers from the garden or hedgerow stood in a vase on the sideboard..On the table was a collection of childish paintings,sheets of scribbled paper,the clothes on the airer were simple,practical and most importantly serviceable.In the in the main room I talked about the different insects,bees,birds,as well as the sudden spurt of flowers in the ankle high grass that I had seen that day.

Fresh air,breathing almost fume free breaths,being able to see for miles,stars that twinkled in the dark indigo sky,unless of course you were cursed with a "pea-souper" of smog which closed out everything except the sound of tawny owls that would twit and twoo across miles of silent countryside.

This was 1950's life...

****

"You can't make a silk purse from a sow's ear"

****

Wherever I went in Gosport there was clean water,dirty water,smelly water,crystal clear water,water to play in,water to play on,water to play with and just plain everyday water.I would walk along the road encroached on by Alver Creek,if the tide was out,at high tide it was only possible to navigate if you wanted wet feet,at times even vehicles couldn't traverse it without a measure of anxiety.I loved to watch the small green crabs with their ungainly sideways movement, creeping amongst the seaweed as the water lapped across the road,oblivious of the risk that were taking from marauding seagulls .When the tide had receded,if they had miscalculated they were likely to go the way of their compatriots whose dried out shells I would stumble over.Their bravado had cost them their lives having become stranded as the tide receded,leaving them to be either baked in the sun or targeted by those ever watchful gulls.I would wander around the shoreline of the clear water of the lake at Gilkicker,paddle my feet in the sea at Stokes Bay as the water ran up the beach, or skim flat stones across the waves to see how many times they would bounce off the surface before inevitably sinking under the surface.Further along the beach,just past the fenced off tennis courts and beach huts there was smelly green stagnant water, the remnants of the old moat,part of the sea defences adjacent to Alver Bank,by the end of the sixties finally filled in,but for now laced with pungent green algae,an ideal summer breeding ground for hordes of small black flies..Apple Dumpling Bridge out at Browndown,afforded litter free clean sparkling water in which I went to play and catch minnows,sticklebacks and in a nearby pool,frog tadpoles.Still further on at Titchfield Haven the reed beds gave me a chance to see the various wetland birds which roosted amongst the tall stems,the short eared owls flying silently above them as dusk set in.The sea wall at Haslar,with its steps down to the water line,the stones and pebbles on the shingle beaches,the creeks and inlets,the dark forbidding moats at Fort Rowner and Fort Brockhurst whose entrance bridges were fenced with barbed wire as they were deemed unsafe.All of them ideal locations for the budding boyhood fisherman.At Walpole Park there were outdoor swimming baths,Gosport Lido, the swinging wooden doors of the changing rooms having a large gap above and below,where mischievous little boys would peek under at the disrobing occupants,bathers teeming around like a plague of ants during the warmth of summer.Nearby was the boating lake and model yacht pond fed from the sea by means of a sluice gate and the venue,every other year for international model yacht races to take place.The beautiful varnished wooden yachts,fully rigged with white sails and resplendent spinnakers arrived with their proud nautical owners,Frenchmen,Belgians,Dutchmen and often sailors from even further afield.If I arrived early in the mornings I could gain employment "crewing"the reward a half a crown or five bob.The only likelihood of me getting wet was from rain or falling in if I overstretched as I guided the large yacht back out to the centre of the pond where they would once more catch the best gusts of wind,At the end of the weeks racing if they had done well in its races I might get given a bonus for my part in their victorious efforts.On many days in summer these various activities passed the time,fresh air,exercise and mostly the attraction of being free! Indeed Gosport had a great deal of water,much of it put to good recreational use.

****

''There's no smoke without fire''

****

''You'll eat anything'' the voice said,''what won't you eat''and it was true,unable to buy the best it occurred to me that half a century later children of my age would starve.Why? Well the items I ate in the mid twentieth century,many of them,are not even seen in the shops anymore,certainly mention the word offal in 2020 and children are horrified..Would they know what''mouse trap cheese''was.Would they scrape the mould off of the stale cheddar,or the white mould off of the top of the homemade strawberry jam,would they eat the blackened toast,slightly burnt then scraped off with a knife or just get another slice and start again.If meat didn't smell ''off'' we used it,maybe just added a bit of extra seasoning.Nothing had a sell by date,if it looked edible you ate it and what was definitely past its use then the pig man would use it for swill.Stale bread was used for bread pudding,a joint of meat was used as the basis for several meals,cold,shepherds pie and stews,spoiled fruit would be used for jams or pies with the unusable pieces cut out or peeled away.

Every housewife knew how to cook,recipes passed from mother to daughter,everything made from the basic ingredients,nothing''ready made''.Where I ask have these things disappeared to,are they now just thrown away or are our pets better fed,I walk down the street,more often than not all alone or surrounded by overfed rotund figures,we throw food away because"its out of date",we obviously eat far more than we need and throw away food unnecessarily purchased, how things have changed,often not always for the better.

****

"Red sky at night shepherd's delight,red sky in morning shepherd's warning"

****

As winter faded away the weather became less chilly,frosty mornings became less frequent and the watery sun which punctuated the April showers tempted me at my peril to venture out coat less."Ne'er cast a clout till May is out", I was often told,more than likely ignored advice.The confusion was as to whether it was referring to the end of that calendar month or the white flowers of the maytree,or hawthorn,being in flower.Nevertheless the brisk breezes that occurred during the ensuing weeks used to provide me with a veritable wealth of entertainment,apart that is from the delight of seeing the clean washing losing its grip on the clothes line on a Monday morning,in order to find its way into a neighbour's garden.Apart from this,with Nana,the ever present matriarch in attendance,I would skip happily down the road as we made our way to Alverstoke.Clouds scurried across the blue and as we entered Green Lane it was noticeably cooler in the shade of the aged horse chestnut trees with their new finery that was just emerging.Leaving the lane by the old Alverstoke Junior School,we passed St.Mary's Church and the National Children's Home, standing on the corner of Clayhall Road, before emerging onto the green adjacent to Gilkicker Lake which was our intended destination.The ripples ran across the lake,fuelled by a light breeze,I threw in a stone and watched the concentric circles move across the water spreading out wider and wider until they exhausted themselves.The tufts of last years grass,now turned brown,were interspersed with new green shoots of spring,bending in the onshore breeze as they lay in the direction of Haslar.On the opposite side of the little single track was a larger area of grass which we were headed for,we quickly found a sheltered spot in the lee of the concrete wall,left over from the endeavours of wartime Gosport and the D-Day Invasion.

For the entire journey I had been tightly clutching a small bundle of sticks,which once joined by the contents of Nana's grey shopping bag became something quite extraordinary.A piece of red,green.blue and yellow cloth was unrolled,then the sticks, which were actually dowel rods,were inserted down the narrow pockets along the edges to form an unequal diamond shape,a kite, on which was a string tail to which bows were attached.A square wooden reel suitably loaded with string,the end of which was attached to the base of the diamond and we were ready to begin.Holding the reel,at the same time feeding out the string, it was Nanas job to hold on to the kite whilst I tugged gently on the line to try to get it to rise up into the sky.As it started to gain height It dipped turned,dived and swerved,the wind began to take me across the grass almost as fast as the kite which I was trying, not entirely successfuly,to stop from entwining itself around the line of a fellow pilot nearby.Thankfully a crash avoided with the other kite,having lost control of my kite it crashed into the ground,thankfully requiring only minor repairs before allowing me to launch it again.After trying several more attempts, the kite actually in the air less time than me,it wasn't long before the kite and its snaking tail proved less entertaining as we became too tired to launch it anymore. Nana,now totally exhausted,after all she was almost seventy years old, needed a rest and it took all of her remaining energy to walk across to the cafe to purchase an ice cream whilst I assembled the other item that was in the shopping bag.In the bag was a simple kit to make a glider.Removing the pieces from the paper sleeve,the kit was made of balsa wood,it was a simple task to slide the wings and tail plane through the slots in the fuselage,then the front end was weighted with a pinched lead weight.Finally assembled I drew my arm back,pointing it up at an angle,with the mightiest of throws I could muster,the glider soared into the sky,only to return to earth after what seemed seconds.It never lasted long,it soon broke and was much more tiring and less successful than the previous kite flying.The next time when we purchased another it had a propeller which could be wound up with an elastic band,supposedly this was meant to be an improvement but it still seemed to crash immediately I launched it.By now Nana and the anticipated ice cream had arrived,so we sat in the shelter afforded by the wall and I chattered happily about the daring flying exploits that the afternoon had provided,not that there had been many,but I did have one last attempted flight,before starting on the weary walk home.

****

"Mighty oaks grow from little acorns"

****

It was Easter Monday,I really longed for some chocolate,but I'd already eaten all of my small Cadbury's chocolate egg the day before.We would only have had one,in spite of being told "don't eat it all at once you'll be sick and once its gone its gone",I would still eat it in one go. The boiled eggs that had been painted had been eaten for breakfast the same day,so whilst my sister had been less impetuous,saving some of her chocolate,I was left with a "beg,borrow or steal scenario".The last two were out of the question,it was not deemed acceptable for them and begging not only frowned upon but was unlikely to succeed,it had been tried before.My outlook was bleak,no desired chocolate,making it worse my sister sat smiling as she ate her saved rations,much to her delight and my dismay.It was a fine day,but the daily chores still had to be done,this was the traditional weekend that saw the prospect of summer sunshine and additionally it was the time to prepare for the better weather to come..Cars were few and far between,they were far too expensive for most ordinary folk, so it meant that walking or cycling were the accepted ways to get around,we were lucky as we had an old black Ford Prefect,"sit up and beg",car,Dad had been part of a football pools syndicate so had used some of his winnings to purchase a second hand car,later to be replaced by a company car,as he progressed from bricklayer to site agent.Whatever your mode of transport it was important to free up the time for those summer forays into the country or down to the beach by preparing for it this weekend.Grandad or Dad would spend the morning darting in and out of the shed,fixing this and that,oil cans in hand,hammers,spanners and glue to effect any necessary repairs,they had to do them themselves as there was no money to pay others to do them.Whilst this took place I kicked my tennis ball around the square of grass or up against the wall in the backyard,remembering acutely the tinkle of glass when the back window had got in the way the previous Easter.Adjacent gardens echoed with children's impish laughter,adults scolding,and over the fence discussions,it was a bank holiday everyone had time off work.Single cylinder hand propelled mowers made their distinctive sounds as they scythed their way across the grass,the final push with the mower tilted upwards so it made that satisfying whirr as it cut through the air.It was accompanied by the chink of a spade as the flower beds were being prepared to receive their colourful bedding plants once the wallflowers were ready to go on the compost heap..Lunch,sorry dinner,over,I would get ready to "go out' ",I never understood it was necessary to be dressed in my "best" clothes when I could be going to the allotments in Middlecroft Lane or simply fishing at Apple Dumpling Bridge.It was almost a prerequisite that wherever you ventured you had to look your best,it was seen as respect and a reflection on your upbringing.Traditionally Grandad planted his seed potatoes this weekend,they had been chitted in the shed in preparation as it "gave them a good start" and whilst he was digging the trench and earthing up I would hunt under the sheets of corrugated tin for the early slow worm.So it was that this particular day I was dressed in the most ludicrous outfit of a white sun hat,pale blue short sleeved cotton shirt,grey flannel shorts,white cotton short socks and brown buckled sandals just to go fishing for tadpoles in the pond at Browndown.The journey up Leesland Road,along to Wilmott Lane and then onto the Military Road seemed endless,but once we arrived at Grange airfield I knew it wasn't too much further.We passed the road track from Grange airfield that they used for the Gosport Speed Trials,when cars like Allard,MG and Triumph were put through their paces, making our way across the edge of the airfield to our destination.Nana was dressed in her Sunday best pushing an old blue pushchair,as almost inevitably I would be too tired to walk home unaided,but surprisingly she didn't appear out of place,others too were dressed in the same...after all it was a bank holiday! As we approached our destination, the old wooden bridge was uncrowded, apart from a few other children poking around with their fishing nets,jam jars with string handles stood by their side full of cloudy water awaiting their inmates,it was fairly deserted.Once filled with either minnows,red and blue,sticklebacks or the odd diving beetle, if I was lucky,tadpoles from one of the nearby pools, we would make our way home,the only distraction being the wildflowers and the birds,in and out of the bushes,starting to build their nests.

****

''Just give them the benefit of the doubt''

****

As I sat in my garden watching the small white fluffy clouds scuttling across the sunny blue sky I couldn't but help to think back to the 1950's when I was growing up.As I enjoyed my outdoor lunch the road outside was again quiet,no loud radios,no screeching tyres,no white vapour trails in a sky which seemed much bluer,less hazy, than it had been most recently.It was almost possible to hear the wings of the Brimstone,Orange Tip and Tortoiseshell butterflies as they danced by, eagerly searching for a nectar meal from one of the nodding flowers..In the distance a yaffle or green woodpecker could be heard drumming on a dead tree trunk,a great tit nearer to home in the garden with its call reminiscent of a bicycle tyre being pumped up was almost drowned out by a chattering group of house sparrows building nests in my eaves.In the pond frogs croaked in unison interspersed by a poignant plop as one noisily entered the water to join his friends.I could hear the new lime green foliage on the oak tree tree rustling in the light breeze as it rippled through the branches.Along the,now silent, road verge I could hear the bumble of large solitary bees and when I listened carefully the rustling movement of rabbits and mice as they moved amongst the wildflowers and brambles that were starting to proliferate.Small birds,even larger magpies, were noisily squabbling as they hurried around starting to build their nests for the coming breeding season.After sixty years it seemed strange that the way we had appreciated nature when I was a small boy,the lack of noise,the more leisurely pace had returned once more,the opportunity for children was there again.

****

''Curiosity killed the cat''

****

I reflected I thought of how happy Easter was.....but then another thought clouded my mood as I became acutely aware that many less fortunate people had failed to make it to today illness had cut short their mortality the same as it had when I was a boy.My thoughts were with those many individuals,whatever race,colour or creed,I shared their sorrow,as I had shared the same sorrow back in the early fifties when polio and tuberculosis had been the scourge of my childhood. We needed to take this opportunity,even in grief to grasp what is freely around you for you and your families to enjoy as we did in those times years before. Most importantly remember that neighbours as well as family can need help,community spirit is of paramount importance,life is not just about the individual,it is about all of us.The 1950's was a good time to grow up...grasp the chance to have this togetherness again,there will be some casualties but out of this crisis let's gain something good and let tomorrow's memories be as good then as ours are now.

****

''All work and no play makes Jack a dull boy''

Sunny days,school holidays were here but what could we do,we had six weeks to amuse ourselves,six weeks with very little spare money so what could I occupy my time doing.My group of friends and I would meet almost every day in Privet Park to play football or cricket.Day after day it became habitual,we needed a change, so we decided to go to natures gym without further ado.Not a gymnasium like we see now but one we could enjoy with what we had at hand Making do with natural things around us we thought of it more as a bit of fun and adventure.We cycled across Grange airfield before disappearing down the muddy track flanked on both sides with yellow prickly gorse bushes.As it opened out onto Browndown the track became sandy and in no time at all we arrived at a clear sparkling stream running under a rickety wooden bridge,the famous Apple Dumpling Bridge.This was the site of our gymnasium and best of all it was free,anyone could turn up,everyone could take part but you mustn't break anything,after all it was borrowed and didn't belong to you.The choice was amazing,the balance bar,the vault,the rope swing,the obstacle course,monkey climb,I could choose what I wanted but where was it.Well I didn't need to look far nature had provided everything I needed for free.A tree branch had a rope attached to provide a rope climb,when a seat was tied to the bottom of it using a piece of branch it served as a swing.The same piece of rope tied between two trees either side of the little stream made a hand bridge,for the braver a tightrope walk,a longer branch laid across the river banks provided a balance bar,both of these items a source of several immersions.small bushes provided vaults for us to jump.the obstacle course was made up of any naturally occurring item that could be pressed into use or was in the way of your running.The point to all this was that if you put your mind to it you could, with sufficient imagination, having everything you desired.

****

''An ounce of prevention is worth a pound of cure''

****

A long piece of string,an old garter that had once held up my long grey school socks,two or three white chicken quill feathers,a wooden clothes peg,and a piece of chalk.My trouser pocket contained them all,along with some more rather obnoxious items which were mostly dead but sometimes still moving as my Nana would testify.From one of my sorties into the countryside I had returned home not unusually with some equally strange items,they consisted of a forked stick,a long straight stick and a slightly shorter one,a couple of rose hips,a conker or two,the hollow stem of a cow parsley plant and a hapless caterpillar that had looked interesting when I found it.By the time I had placed the items on the lawn in the garden the caterpillar had unfortunately gone to its maker,however,shamefully,it was still of some amusement as I deposited its remains down my sisters blouse.The screams were worth the effort as she gave up her daisy chain making and her fixation with putting a buttercup under my chin to decide if "I liked butter"and ran off in doors shouting "I'm telling dad about you".Taking the remaining items from my pocket I placed them with the other pieces from the recent country walk which I had collected.There was one item missing to complete the picture, before I could begin to make use of all the items a small penknife that Grandad had given me to use when we were at his allotment had to be found.Having retrieved the small knife from the garden shed I was able to begin turned the various oddments into useful items,well to me useful to others more of a annoyance.The forked stick once fitted with my garter made an extremely efficient catapult,the string I then cut in half,one half of which I strung the conker onto,knotting the end so it didn't fall off.Taking the longer piece of string I then tied it taut to either end of the longer of the two sticks.Meanwhile the smaller stick was sharpened at one end,the other end being slit to take the feathers and I had a serviceable bow and arrow.The clothes peg,once a face had been added,made a figure to go in one of my toy cars,alternatively it would be a doll for my sister at ChristmasThe hollow plant stem became a very accurate pea shooter,the rose hip once cut open had a very effective itching powder inside and the piece of chalk was used on the pavement to mark out the numbers for a game of hopscotch or to mark a trail of arrows so my friends could

follow me if I had left home before them.The total cost to me,nothing except time,the effort hardly any at all,the result enough items of toys to while away a good deal of my spare time.Cheap and easy to make,easy to replace,I had very little but turned it into a lot maybe those times will return again.

****

"An apple a day keeps the doctor away"

****

In the 1950's my Grandad used to have a pint of bitter in this pub every dinner time,it was a daily ritual,that he never missed, he was in his 70's and I used to stand at the door of The Junction public house to try and peek in should the opportunity arriive.It was one of those events that the excitement was generated by the sole fact that you were looking at something you shouldn't be.There was something behind those doors I wasn't meant to see but that meant I must try to see it.Peeking through the partly open door,beery smoke laden air filtering out,a tap would come on my shoulder,a gruff voice would say"what you up to young man" and sheepishly I would run away to a safer distance to wait for grandad to emerge.In those days public houses were frugally furnished, inside it was dowdy and basic,wooden stools,scruffy chairs and scratched tables stood on the grubby beer stained floor boards,a covering of sawdust making it easy to clean up the spillages,not always beer,but sometimes blood when a couple of drinkers had mixed opinions,it was typical"spit and sawdust"a working man's pub!

****

"You can't judge a book by it's cover"

Several days had passed since I had been standing watching the circus parade,the weekend had passed and on my one visit to the high street I had to pass by Walpole Park.All the vehicles associated with the circus were parked around the sides of the green and at the rear of a huge high tent supported by four enormous poles and a network of twisted wire cables,predominantly it was white but the walls of it were red and white vertical segments like planks of wood.At the front was a short tunnel providing an entrance stood next to which was a slightly tatty,off white caravan,the ticket office,a constant small queue waiting for it to open to buy a ticket or two for a matinee or evening performance.I never asked to go,the reply was rarely encouraging but this time was different as I was going to have a chance to go,not with dad but with Nana.Dad,as normal, was busy,but with the poster in his shop window had come a small reward,in return for displaying the advertising poster he had been given four tickets for the Friday evening performance,I was going to the show with Nana,Grandad and my cousin,Melvyn.Walking across Walpole Park I was able to see the elephants tethered by their legs to large stakes hammered into the ground,the odd roar from a big cat,no not a ginger tom,a lion or tiger, punctuated the air,as did the neighing of the ponies and barking of the dogs.At certain times of day the animals could be viewed in their quarters behind the big top at an additional fee.It was rather like an exotic zoo, although the conditions the animals lived in were far from ideal,they were clean but had very restricted movement and many had a look of boredom.Arriving at the entrance tunnel a giant man on stilts towered over us,an exotically dressed usherette took the tickets and then led us to or hard seats.The wooden tiered seats ran right around the huge tent,sitting on them you could see the grass underneath,the ring was covered with a layer of sawdust the only thing separating the audience from the artists a ring of wooden boxes in red and blue about two feet high.High above the ring were various trapezes,a tight rope and above the tunnel the performers entered from a huge colourful cannon.The floodlights picked out various areas depending on who was in the ring,the lion tamer cracked his whip,the lions cowered,and he put his head in one of the felines mouths,it looked dangerous but realistically was probably not.Clowns came in and out,custard pies flew thick and fast as the comic figures with big red noses,enormous shoes,loose fitting garments and hats crowned with flowers fell,tripped and spurred the audience into hilarity.A posse of wild west characters performed bareback on ponies.Dogs,pigeons,camels and those huge elephants all performed in various ways under the undivided attention of the red coated ringmaster in his black boots,top hat and far reaching whip.A row of sequin clad girls lay across the ring as the elephants stepped carefully over them before sitting on large wooden circular half barrel platforms.Acrobats swung high above on trapezes and sometimes themselves,the tightrope walker journeyed high across the ring,even the clowns muscled in to cause organised chaos,all without a safety net.The only time a safety net was used was to catch the projectile from the cannon,a person dressed as a human cannonball.Performance completed,performers and audience stood to sing "God save the Queen" then filed out in silence to face the falling darkness of the evening.

****

'There's a method in his madness"

****

Respects had been paid,the mourners having returned for the last time to 80 Leesland Road tried very hard to comfort me,but it didn't make much difference to how I felt, they didn't understand what the day meant to me.The finality of that last journey,on that afternoon had taken away not only my best friend,but my"mum"and my trusted advisor and confidant,I no longer had anyone there who I could turn to,I was on my own for the first time in my life.When everyone eventually left,their words, "you'll be alright lad" ringing in my ears,"keep your spirits up",the silence suddenly became so real.The little terrace house that had given me so much had become unusually silent,when I left that day what was ahead I didn't have any idea,except the prospect of being lonely.The times when voices chattered and happy laughter rang around the tiny rooms was gone forever,no more Boxing Day parties,or hot buttered toast round the open fire,no more Nana's cottage pie,no more homemade still lemonade,all of it gone forever,all that was left were the memories.As the last people and immediate family left,the door banged shut for the last time.I too left for home,tears in my eyes,a misty glaze fogging my view,my route not without a detour to Ann's Hill Cemetery to gaze and shed a tear beside the grave,marvel at the colourful wreaths and flowers piled on the earth mound under which the now empty body lay,How much she was loved and missed the spirit I knew gone I know not where,hopefully to the heaven she had religiously prepared for all of her mortal life.

 The following week the remaining members of the family met back at 80 Leesland Road,no longer a home,just a place to empty out and dispose of the vestiges of a life that no longer had a meaning.Was all that scrimping and saving,making ends meet, hard work,pain,suffering and disappointment all that there was.When the house was locked for the last time that day,all I had in my hand was a few trinkets nobody else wanted,my riches however were in the memories that I still have today.

After that day I rarely saw my uncle or cousins again,my father had never been overly friendly towards any of them and although outwardly very affable was not of a gregarious nature.With this in mind it was inevitable that life became a solitary and often isolated period for me,due to circumstances old friends drifted away and I found making others was not to be an easy task.

****

''Many hands make light work''

****

Having gone to Portsmouth Grammar School it was not easy to make or establish friendships because of the geographical proximity to pupils in my class,I now lived in Rowner they nearly all lived in Portsmouth.I tried relentlessly to continue my primary school relationships but it became harder and harder,my friends school culture at Brune Park was so very different to that I was experiencing.I was becoming a person who just dropped in,a casual acquaintance,the daily contact was no longer possible.The friends I did have were discouraged from coming to Masten Crescent to "call for me",they were viewed as a nuisance,so much so that they stopped coming,they were never allowed in and felt that they were unwelcome..My sister had married and moved away with her new family,eventually emigrating to Australia.Dad was always occupied with his never ending pursuit of money,he was either at John Hunts,where he was a site agent, or in his grocer's shop in Rowner Lane.He was never really at home,he never really noticed that I was not welcome in the new family and every effort it seemed was made to keep me away and out of mind..

****

The early bird always catches the worm"

****

It was a lovely summer's day and the sun was shining from a cloudless blue sky as we turned out of the hospital car park and ascended the steep hill in order to join the narrow road that ran along the top of Portsdown Hill.It was little wider than a country lane as we passed Fort Widley and Fort Purbrook,overlooking Portsmouth Harbour as they had done since Queen Victoria's reign.To the northern side of the hill lay Southwick House,an imposing white building set in lovely parkland,as with the forts,it secretly guarded its part in wartime adventures,it's rooms had been privy to the planning of one of the greatest military operations ever seen,General Eisenhower's HQ,the nerve centre of the D-Day landings.To the south of the chalk cliff,a sloping grassy scrub covered bank overlooked the City of Portsmouth,Portsmouth Harbour and in the distance across the Solent,the Isle of Wight.As the panoramic views unfolded the short grass on the edge of the roadside verges was alive with the steady hum of myriads of insects.They wandered and flew through the chalkland vegetation,searching for sustenance amongst the vetches,trefoil,thyme,eyebright and my favourite the wild orchids.As the road widened a little approaching the belisha beacon crossing which ran between the wire fencing of the ASWE compounds belonging to the Ministry of Defence,it afforded great protection to the exotic rarities of our natural orchids nestled in the short sheep grazed grass I caught tantalising glimpses of bee,monkey and spider orchids,whose blooms

82

had replaced the purple,spotted and pyramid which had flowered much earlier,only glimpses as it was prohibited to stop because of military security guards.It was an ideal habitat as they were well protected from the public eye by virtue of the security of the sensitive site.Descending the winding lane past Fort Nelson,unused and lying idle we bent our necks to peer up at the bust of Lord Nelson at the very top of Nelson's Column, a reminder of the great admiral who had been victorious at the Battle of Trafalgar. It was here that we turned left down what was almost a cart track,full of potholes,very narrow and very steep,this was Pigeon House Lane.The grassy chalk verges were now replaced by dusty chalk covered and stunted shrubby bushes,blackthorn,hawthorn and the rosy pink blossoms of the dog rose flowers,a wild variety echoing the belief of some that the world was only seen in this way,"through rose coloured spectacles"that nothing of a gloomy nature ever stayed in our thoughts or memories.The T- junction at the bottom of the hill led us back once more on to the main A27 carriageway,by turning to the right we cycled past the Delme Arms public house,turned under the viaduct which crossed the River Wallington as it joined Fareham Creek before wearily pedalling up the small steep incline which passed the little garage and the Red Lion hotel before heading into West Street Fareham.Turning left passing the old fire station we once again went under the viaduct,the collier moored at the coal yard came into view resting on the mud of the smelly creek,we were heading home and it seemed a very long way.By now it was late afternoon and the factories in Gosport Road were emptying their workforces,there were few cars but an endless throng of pedestrians and cyclists all rushing in their haste to get home.Gratefully we turned down Wych Lane,cycles passing us on every side,under the narrow railway arch,passed Bridgemary secondary school and at the Wych Way Inn turned into Rowner Lane for the final leg home.At Rowner crossroads my friend and I parted ways,he leaving to cycle to his home in Bury Close, me leaving to return the short distance left to mine, hoping that nobody asked where I had been,I had been out all afternoon but only I knew where I had been.The weekend that followed passed uneventfully,Monday arrived to herald a new week,after my normal breakfast,I rode my bike down to Privet Park and spent the morning playing football with my friends,on my return to home from the park at lunchtime I was met with a strange empty silence.Something wasn't normal,but what was the reason,there was a sombre mood,it was as though I already knew,"is Nana dead" I asked,the reply a faint "Yes".I didn't cry,I felt numb,I quickly went to my bedroom and sat on the edge of my bed,the day I had dreaded had arrived and I was on my own,the future slightly uncertain my thoughts in turmoil.The next few days were like living in a bad dream,I tried hard to understand what had occurred but constantly my thoughts returned to me never seeing Nana ever again.Before I knew the day of the funeral was upon me and I was determined I mustn't let Nana down,after all she had done so much for me,now it was my chance to start to repay the debt in some small way.We assembled at 80 Leesland Road,the curtains were drawn, the coffin had traditionally laid overnight in the parlour,it was being used by Nana,to rest for the last time before she set off on the start of her final journey.Croslands the local funeral directors arrived headed by Eddie Crosland,he respectfully secured the lid on the coffin then removed the casket,placing it in the gleaming black hearse waiting outside waiting to transport the polished oak coffin to St. Faith's Church in Tribe Road.Nana had been a member of the congregation there for many years,it was fitting that she should be leaving through its doors that final day,Me,I had last visited the church several months before and today was to be no exception,I couldn't endure the pain of that finality.The choice was mine,nobody else's and I chose not to go that day,I knew that Nana would understand,she always had, so I waited on her scrubbed doorstep for the last time.Around me,heads bowed,respectfully subdued were the many friends and neighbours she had lived amongst for many years,Mrs King,Miss Read,Miss Raggett,Mrs Lucas.Mr and Mrs Horne,Mrs Sands,Mrs Pavey,Mrs Lawrence,Mr and Mrs Edwards the Shepherds,the Weavers,Mr and Mrs Clogg,Auntie Ada,Uncle Bert,Auntie Amy,another Auntie Ada there were so many.They walked up Leesland Road following the cortege to the final internment at Ann's Hill cemetery where she would join her husband Charlie next to her only daughter Audrey,my mum.As the gleaming black hearse,followed by two limousines appeared,it was led on its way by Eddie Crosland,impeccably dressed as always,walking a respectful distance in front,at the sedate pace dictated by a funeral procession.It slowed, paused momentarily in front of the small Victorian terraced house to bid its own silent farewell.Onlookers bowed their uncovered heads,a mark of respect,crossed themselves,the action accompanied by a few stifled sobs and tears,but none were mine.I had promised myself I wouldn't let her down by crying and I didn't.As the cortege moved further on,the undertaker returned to his car,the hearse moved slowly up Leesland Road.acknowledging the gathered mourners that lined the street and I quietly retreated into the silent interior of number 80 to await the return of the mourners from the graveside.I would return only once more after today only to finish the final chapter in that part of my life and to cross that doorstep to the house I had regarded as home for one last time.

****

"They are just like two peas in a pod"

****

Some people thought it was brave to cycle from Gosport to Queen Alexandra Hospital at Cosham,a not particularly short or easy journey.Brave..No...Tiring..Very.In the early sixties life's pace was slower,traffic lighter and drivers more considerate.You felt safe when you walked or cycled the streets and people in the vast majority could be trusted.There were bobbies on the beat,"if your lost ask a policeman",people were friendly and spoke to each other,people looked after each other.Brave...No we just lived at a less selfish time or maybe just on another planet!

****

"Take what he says with a grain of salt"

****

The next morning was Friday,melancholy was the order of the day,it was the sense of "not knowing",the sense of lingering,waiting for the inevitable ending but not knowing when it would come,hoping all the time that it wouldn't,that it was just a bad dream..I remember several times asking"when can we go and see Nana in hospital",no thought entering my mind that it might already be too late,the faint hope that the door would open and in she would walk.It was almost as though she had gone on holiday,Ijust didn't comprehend hospital and death."I don't know" was the reply"we'll have to wait and see".Quietly I crept out to make my way to Privet Park to meet my friends,the ride on my bicycle,I performed in a rather preoccupied manner,should I really be going at all I asked myself, what should I do next,tomorrow was the weekend so it was unlikely we would visit the hospital then.I couldn't help thinking of Nana on her own, waiting until Monday was a long time,even then there was every chance that I wouldn't be allowed to go in as there was a tendency to discourage children in hospitals.
As I arrived at the park,I met up with my friends but football was not

uppermost in my thought and my lack of enthusiasm soon became evident from my half hearted participation in the game.As I went and sat on the grass,being no more than a hindrance to the other players, my best friend at the time,who had been with me the day before when we saw the ambulance in Newgate Lane ran over to enquire after my well being.I relayed the events of the previous evening and mentioned that it was my intention to ride to Cosham that afternoon to Queen Alexandra Hospital to see my Nana".I'll come with you" he said.So glad of the chance of company I arranged to meet at Brockhurst after our lunch,neither of us thought that although as children we were very unlikely to be allowed entrance when we arrived at our destination that we wouldn't be able to find a way in.

The afternoon was sunny.not too hot,with a cooling breeze blowing in our faces as we pedalled briskly along Fareham Road,over the railway crossing at Bedenham Gates that led to the navy armament depots at Frater and Bedenham,and then approached The North Star public house.On the left was the aircraft towing route,it ran along Tichborne Way,and was used to move aircraft from HMS Daedalus,in the past it was moving aircraft from Grange Airfield where in the early fifties the Gosport Motor Speed Trials had taken place.By the railway gates it joined the road we were on before making its final approach to Fleetlands Royal Naval Repair yard.I eyed with a cold hateful stare the dentist's surgery which was located in one of the bungalows,where I had had a tooth removed by a butcher who revelled in blood letting.On the opposite of the road stood the little post office with its steady flow of customers from the surrounding factories,Passing the narrow road junction with Wych Lane, we glimpsed the traffic lights controlling the traffic as it passed under the narrow railway arch.The houses were now only on one side of the road,the other the site of various factories,Osmiroid producing fountain pens,Lederle,later Cyanamide,who manufactured chemicals,Ultra the home of wireless and radio.As they went out of view,we rode down the dip in the road,over the little stream,all that was visible of the ford,before climbing up the hill to pass the Hoeford Public House next to the Provincial bus depot,behind the car showroom.Continuing on towards Fareham Creek,as was usual,smelling of gaseous mud and green algae,we then passed under the railway viaduct,glimpsing Gibson's metal foundry as we cycled up to West Street.Turning right into West Street over the traffic lights,the Red Lion Hotel,once a coaching inn, appeared in view before we headed under the Viaduct once more,before passing Cams Alders Estate as we joined the A27.We cycled into Porchester,not much more than a village,the castle visible on the shoreline of the creek in the distance.Leaving the little village centre we encountered the tempting smell of Smiths potato crisps wafting from the factory situated opposite the Castle Trading Estate,its white lorries with their blue and white crisp packet logo.Further along on the shoreline stood the Blue Star Garage with its small "greasy spoon" cafe,a favourite of builders,following on to the slightly noxious smell of pharmaceuticals which came from Johnson and Johnson's factory where they made Cussons talcum powder.Cycling on we turned left up the steady climb towards the entrance to the hospital,on arrival we leant our bikes against a wall,soon locating the ward in which Nana was residing.I walked nervously,with my equally nervous friend,along the well polished floor of the quiet corridor,everyone spoke in whispered voices,each sparsely furnished ward holding several heavy metal beds,occupied by sick patients being cared for.Each ward running either side of the corridor was entered by a partially glazed door,each bed had a white cabinet next to it on which stood a carafe of water and a glass.The bed was basic,made up with crisp clean white linen,a clipboard was fixed to the foot,a name tag and"nil by mouth" posted at the head with very little else to be seen,except the white curtains surrounding some of the beds.White and blue uniformed nurses would appear,then disappear just as quickly.We eventually arrived at the entrance to the ward we wanted,I pushed the door open,a nurse and matron glanced across and asked what we wanted,my reply was that I was visiting my Nana and I had cycled from Gosport.They asked her name,explaining that children were not normally allowed in,as we already were aware,but as an act of kindness and compassion they said that if we were quiet we could have five minutes.I nervously followed the rather intimidating matron to a basic bed on which lay Nana.She didn't stir, as I reached out my hand I felt a light gentle squeeze on mine and wearily her eyes flickered open. I told her who was with me,and a ghostly attempt at a smile flickered on her face.With no words,far too weak to say anything she had drifted back to her sedated sleep,it was time to go."I'll be back next week" I said,as we whispered goodbye,knowing this was probably to be last time,next week was not to come and as things turned out it wouldn't be necessary to come again, my expectations having been met.

****

"Just throwing good money after bad"
I lay in bed,straining my ears,desperately trying to interpret the muffled voices which I could hear coming from downstairs,I even crept to the bedroom door and listened intently through the opening but all to no avail.Once back in bed I lay slightly bewildered as to the strange events that had occurred that day,but as those voices stopped and I heard the front door close my eyes closed too and I drifted into an uneasy slumber.Uncle Dennis had left to ride home to his house in Alverstoke,something had been agreed but I wasn't to learn what that was until the morning.The following morning another balmy summer's day was promised as the early morning sun streamed across the back

garden,beans on toast for breakfast and after looking in on Nana,who was still asleep,I snatched my silver paper bundle,my lunch for the day,from the kitchen."Don't be late for tea"said a voice as I climbed on my bicycle,scooted down the drive and opened the black scrolled iron gate which I carefully latched behind me. As I cycled up the slight incline and around the bend in Rowner Lane as I went past the parish church my mind was set on where we would end up once I had met up with the others at a pre arranged point at Brockhurst.I turned right,past the garage and its busy workshop at the Rowner Road junction and headed towards Rowner Arch,when to my delight I saw my group of friends coming towards me having decided to come up and meet me as I rode down.I quickly spun my bike around in the road and pulled up until they had joined me.

After a brief consultation,we decided we would head towards Titchfield Haven,so riding slowly along Rowner Road,past Newgate Lane,then the bungalows which were opposite the naval airfield we chatted happily as we made our way almost aimlessly in that direction.It was tempting to stop and watch through the fence at the aircraft that were on the base,but almost as soon as you stopped a Military Police Land Rover would approach from inside the perimeter fence requesting you to "move on please".The memories of previous conflicts were still fresh, in people's minds,the growing threat of Russia and the escalation of the "cold war" were uppermost in the minds of the security forces,meaning even we children were not above suspicion,particularly with our Kodak Brownies slung around our necks!

Disappearing from view,we approached the church and ancient village green at Stubbington,but before actually entering the little village we turned left back towards Lee on the Solent.After a few hundred yards a right turn took us down Monk's Hill, lined with its lofty scots pines and high sandy banks which framed our first glimpses of the Solent,the stretch of water between us and the Isle of Wight.Descending towards the beach we could catch the first glimpse of any oil tankers and transatlantic liners leaving Southampton Water,a rare treat as there were very few in comparison to modern times,to us they were enormous but if seen today,almost no bigger than the size of a Gosport

Ferry in comparison!.

We paused for a while on the beach eager to explore the sandy shore whilst the tide was out,at the water's edge we searched for any sign of life,skimmed stones or collected various sea shells,cockle,winkle,whelk and the very pretty topshells and turret shells.Walking back up the shore,sand on our shoes,the salt water when it dried leaving white marks on our footwear,resulting in a scolding later on arrival back home.We watched the little spurts of water coming from holes that suddenly appeared in the wet sand under which the living cockles were hidden,frantically we dug down with our bare hands to try and retrieve one,elsewhere razor shells occasionally rose vertically from

the silt and sand.Before remounting our bicycles we would have a swift drink from our water bottles,then ride on to the sluice gate at the haven where the river met the sea,by which time we were ready to stop for lunch.Sitting on the grass,next to the wooden sluice,it was so silent in the warm sun,apart from faint splashing as the water trickled through the ancient leaking gates,a gentle breeze rustling in the reed beds,the odd waterfowl,maybe a moorhen,breaking the silence.I with my friends,as we devoured our meat paste or jam sandwiches,would marvel at the variety that nature provided,all of us aware of the jewels which we were invited to get a glimpse of,the odd word from one of us as a new treasure was spotted.I lay with the others on the green sward and gazed up at the cloudless blue sky,oblivious to all but the lilting song of the soaring skylark,so high up it was out of sight until it suddenly dropped into view,the odd quack of a mallard or sometimes the exciting "boom" of a hidden bittern.

Well rested,it was so idyllic that it was an effort at times to eventually start on our way again,me and one friend heading towards Titchfield,past the abbey and then home via Fareham,the others in our group returning the way we had arrived,not wishing to travel any further.Having passed through Titchfield village,fascinated as ever by its beautiful stone abbey ruins and its quaint houses the route took us along"the main road" back into Fareham where we turned into Redlands Lane.Arriving at its junction with Fareham Road,the road leading to Gosport,we were able to see the heavy horses used to draw the milk floats standing in the yard at Tom Parkers Dairy,soon to be completely replaced by impersonal electric vehicles.We forked right to turn into Newgate Lane the last leg before meeting Rowner Road and home.The lane was lined with scruffy fields and hedgerows on both sides until you met the site of HMS Collingwood,where a naval sentry stood on the gate,smartly dressed in navy blue uniform,white blancoed belt and gaiters,highly polished black boots and a white cap emblazoned with a ribbon saying HMS Collingwood..

Just past this naval establishment the road approached the start of the area known as Peel Common,most of the houses lined the right hand side of the road,along with a grocer's shop and a small garage which looked as if it was in somebody's back garden shed.There were a few houses,standing behind the fields on the left but the most prominent building situated at the end of a potholed,gravel track was a green corrugated tin mission hut,"the tin tabernacle".If you carried on down past this edifice you eventually arrived at Peel Farm. It was as we were approaching the bend,with the green corrugated mission hut in sight,that you encountered in the fields in front of it with their ponies and horses grazing happily,an enormous blue and white sign advertising The Belle Vue Hotel in Lee on the Solent,years before known to me as the "Belly View",just opposite the corner shop[later a

Volvo garage],that something happened.

Coming towards me I remember saying to my friend that day as the cream coloured Bedford Ambulance approached us and went silently past,"my Nana's in that".It was like panic took over,my previously weary legs became invigorated,I cycled furiously down Rowner Road,as I approached Rowner Lane I cut the corner yelling"see you later"to my friend.As I crashed through the black scrolled iron gates of the driveway,I threw down my bicycle,rushed through the kitchen and up the hallway,there was silence.It was a deafening silence,the little bedroom door was open,I half entered,the bed was devoid of linen,the bed was empty,the room was empty,I stood and stared,she had gone,I had been right,it had been her in the ambulance,my confusion was complete,what would happen now,what would happen next.

****

"Save something later for a rainy day"

****

The school holidays were only a few days old and it was a typical July day,birds singing in the trees,a cloudless sky and the light haze gradually disappearing with the temperature rising as the sun rose over the little copse.The only likely loud noise to be heard,the rotor blades of a naval helicopter taking off from the airfield at HMS Daedalus,so as I mounted my trusty pale blue Raleigh bicycle the prospects for the day looked good.I rode down Rowner Lane,turned right opposite the church,with its two thatched cottages, and made my way across to the dirt track that crossed Grange Airfield and came out on Military Road.Turning right and then left into Privet Road I continued along the road until I arrived at the park entrance and turned in through the green gates,which the park keeper locked at dusk and reopened at dawn,to find several of my friends were already there and had started to pick teams for a makeshift football game.Getting off my bike I was told what team to join and quickly threw myself full of enthusiasm into the fray, but not for long,it soon had far less appeal as the temperature rose along with the sun.The football game slowly ground to a halt,it was too hot and tiring,the heat sapped your energy and soon all that remained was a group of kids idly lounging on the grass discussing what to do or where to go next.

By the time we had made up our minds that Stoke's Bay was a good prospect it was time to disband for lunch,so with wildly ridden cycles and dawdling pedestrians making their way home for the midday repast,it was agreed to meet up at nearby Stanley Park,in the dell by Alverbank before going to the beach. .

Cycling like a demon to get home,there was no time to be lost in having some food before returning in the afternoon. I turned into our drive,propped up my cycle on the bungalow wall and ran through the backgate and backdoor into the kitchen.There was no visible signs of movement so I walked through the kitchen,up the hall and gently opened the door to the small blue bedroom which was now occupied by Nana.The district nurse had visited whilst I had been out and changed her dressing,the horrible smell from the open cancer wound was,at least temporarily gone,she had been given her medication,had had a wash to freshen her up so she now lay sleeping.She looked so peaceful with her silver hair in its hairnet recently brushed, the quiet tranquility as she lay propped up on a pillow in her blue dressing gown belied the underlying constant pain..

I didn't wish to disturb her,but as she had drifted off to sleep the small grey handbag that she always had at hand had decanted its contents onto the bed along with her wire framed reading glasses.I gently leant forward to retrieve the items in order to return them to the bag and put the glasses on the bedside table but in doing so disturbed her from her slumber,she awoke with a start,somewhat dazed and believing me to be in the process of stealing her bag and its contents.

The ensuing raised voices and resulting chaos alerted my step mother who was coming downstairs from where she had been changing the babies nappy.She told me to go out as she tried to calm the situation,"I'll speak to your father when he gets home your sandwich is on the side in the kitchen."she said,for what reason she needed to speak to dad I was unsure,I certainly,in my view had done nothing wrong. Making my way to the kitchen I carried my sandwich and a glass of water to the dining table,realising that dinner at twelve o'clock was now lunch,teatime replaced by the evening meal,a long standing tradition had changed almost overnight due to distances being travelled to work and school."Out with the old,in with new" in more than one way!

Quickly eaten,some would say bolted,my simple sandwich and glass of water would sustain me till I returned home at five o'clock, so with no further ado I shouted "I'm off",ran out, jumped on my cycle and was on my way.The prospect of playing around on the beach at Stoke's Bay was exciting,that was where we would undoubtedly head when we met up again,but the memory of Nana's reaction,the thought that I was thought to be stealing from her was on my mind,my awareness of how dementia worked was to be a frightening new experience for me.Once at Stanley Park the afternoon progressed as usual with a wander over to Stokes Bay where we lounged about before returning to Alverbank to purchase a penny ice lolly,or an"ice pole".The afternoons events had supplanted my lunchtimes ordeal,so on arriving home I paid a timorous visit to Nana's bedroom and was met with a weak smile and whispered greeting.I sat holding her pale,weak,listless hand for a while and remember the gentle squeeze of reassurance before her fatigue took over once more.I bid her goodnight,ate my evening meal and retired to my bedroom to read,Dad arrived home but by now the threat from lunchtime had been forgotten.Tomorrow would be another day,I new the doctor was due to make a house visit,from the whispered conversations that had been taking place,so with my uncle's arrival well I went upstairs to bed feeling that the outcome of that visit might not be a happy one.

****

''It's nothing more than a storm in a teacup''

****

Autumn had arrived with a blast,an icy blast,even with my black,yellow and red striped school scarf wrapped around my neck and covering my mouth,my warm breath still turned to mist as it met the colder frosty air.Likewise my hands swathed in thick woollen gloves felt little warmer affording little heat to,my fingertips which still froze whilst I waited at the bus stop.The sight of the green Provincial number 7 bus was exceedingly welcome,although it was only a little warmer inside than out on the pavement,but only a little. With a heavy school bag and briefcase to carry,I threw both into the luggage space under the stairs before climbing to the top deck which was almost airless,filled with a smoky haze due to nearly all of the top deck passengers exhaling vast volumes of cigarette smoke,them not being able to smoke on the downstairs deck.

The bus,often overladen,as many passengers as possible crammed on,some riding on the rear platform,in spite of the conductor repeatedly informing the waiting queue,''no more please''.With standing room only on the bottom deck,we lumbered down Rowner Road before approaching the junction at Brockhurst where our route took us through Elson on the way to the Crossways.I remember well the pleasant smell of fresh baked bread from Green's bakery as we pulled up at the bus stop outside the Windsor Castle public house.From the Crossways,passing the Salvation Army Hall.opposite the public conveniences and into Lees Lane, Ashleys,later Sandersons, wallpaper factory was visible on the left as we crossed the railway line into Whitworth Road.I nostalgically glanced at Leesland School as we picked up passengers at the nearby bus stop outside the old Central School.Gordon Road,Foster Gardens,Stoke Road,then the final leg along Gosport High Street to the Ferry Gardens before the arctic crossing of Portsmouth Harbour.The pattern rarely changed,thankfully the weather did,although the prospect of another seven years of the journey was not inviting,particularly as school was a six day ordeal.Yes,every Saturday as well as Monday to Friday was a school day.

****

''It must be once in a blue moon''

****

The maisonette above 101 Rowner Lane continued to shrink in size as more space was needed for the new baby,so after school and during the holidays I would find myself at my Nanas.Even after the move was made to Masten Crescent and I had my own upstairs bedroom it was still far from comfortable as I had to share it with a baby's cot,once it was old enough to sleep outside of Dad's room.At every opportunity,I took any chance I could to go out either down to 80 Leesland Road at

Nana's house.Sometimes it was only in the woods at the end of the garden,its marshy ground sprouting yellow irises and the brackish pond,which was behind the churchyard of St Mary's Church,teemed with wildlife.I often lay on the patchy grass and watched with fascination the newts that swam along the leaf strewn bottom under the sun dappled surface of the muddy pond.I spent as little time at home as possible,Dad was always working,I was discouraged from going into the shop.even if he was there and as Dad was a site agent at John Hunts[builders],his main employment,he wasn't normally there till closing time at six o'clock.The baby at home took up my stepmothers every minute and so the managing of the shop became the task of Mrs Goodall.who had worked there ever since it had opened.My sister had married by now and as Nana became weaker from the cancer,imposition on her became less reasonable.It was at this point that compassion did at least find a tiny foothold as soon my best friend was to depart from their earthly shackles.It was just before the school holidays when I alighted from the number 7 bus at Harcourt Road and walked up to the door of number 80 Leesland Road.I pushed up the sash window,as I always did,removed the key from the cill and as I opened the door the unpleasant smell of the insidious cancer pervaded my nostrils as always..Walking up the passage to the tiny living room,Nana was sat in her well worn armchair,she was obviously in pain,the smell was overpowering and she had been getting weaker for some time,but she still managed a weak smile and an even weaker greeting.I knew she couldn't stay like this any longer, all alone,struggling to look after herself,what to do however was a different question.We sat and drank a cup of tea and we ate a slice of cake,well,at least I did,she had not been eating properly for some while.Unsure of what to do I made my way to the red telephone box at the end of the road and rang firstly my dad,then Uncle Dennis,explaining to them the situation that had unfolded.My uncle quickly arrived and soon after my Dad,after a brief discussion it was decided that she would come to Masten Crescent and have the downstairs bedroom my sister had vacated as the pain and dementia were taking their toll.The stay wasn't to be long however as a few days later she was to be admitted to Queen Alexandra's Hospital at Cosham.The end was close,I saw her one final time after she was taken there,that time she never even recognised me and as she drew her last breath,I lost my last refuge to retreat to.

****

"You can lead a horse to water but you can't make it drink"

****

A typical autumn morning greeted me as I opened the curtains to reveal drops of rain racing down the glass,as a new drop landed to dislodge another rivulet the view outside was crystal clear.The spotlessly clean glass was slightly misted in the corners,it was wet but also cold,it was inevitable it was raining,yesterday Ihad watched Nana sat on the upstairs window sill of the sash windows cleaning outside in a manner viewed as suicidal fifty years on.That was yesterday,today was shopping day and we had to go to town,because it was raining made no difference we still had to eat and a little rain did no harm,just made you uncomfortable.

Out in the road rainwater ran devoid of litter along the gutters and own the cast iron manholes,like a mini waterfall it fell into the drain water in the bottom.As we passed on our way to board a number seven bus in Whitworth Road we were well protected against the cold rain that fell like stair rods and in the gusts of wind stung your face and reddened your cheeks as it stung my skin.Like two fishermen we arrived at the bus stop,Nana in galoshes and raincoat,her bonnet covered held on with a plastic rain hat tied under her chin,her main defence a battered old black umbrella which she constantly watched to see it didn't blow inside out.I was ready to go to sea dressed in black rubber boots,a black gabardine mackintosh secured with a belt around the waist,the sou;wester on my head constantly dripping as the rain run off it.Once at the bus stop we just prayed it wouldn't arrive late,there was no shelter unless you could squeeze under the porch of a house or the door of one of the shops.When the bus arrived in a shower of spray we jumped back as the water was splashed up from the gutter,having ran from any shelter we had found,if you were too late the bus would just continue on its way.Climbing aboard I was greeted with a warm musty damp smell emanating from the passengers aboard,the cloth seats wet and uncomfortable from previous occupants.

The bus pulled up at the library,as we alighted the discomfort of the dampness went with us,raindrops bounced off of the pavements,vehicles splashed us as the parked and when we arrived at Arnett's the fishmongers in North Street the shutters were closed,the normally open fronted shop had just a door open,the rain was so heavy the fish would have swum off the marble counter.Nana and I walked at different speeds so in my attempts to stay under the umbrella the drips from it ran down my neck,meanwhile the drips from the hem of my mac ran into my rubber boots.As we walked down the high street it was almost deserted,the people that were visible quickly disappeared into shops,whose doorways were littered with sheltering shoppers.Dewhurst,Liptons,The Maypole,their shop blinds open even in the rain giving you more obstacles to avoid as the water ran off to ambush the careless pedestrian.Arriving at the bus stand clutching a soggy paper bag,the doughnut in it in danger of falling through it into a puzzle the final gauntlet had to be run.The wind blowing across

Portsmouth Harbour drove the rain like arrows across the parking lots,the buses themselves swayed as the wind caught them broadside,the umbrella turned inside out,I slipped on the bus step and it was the perfect end to a days shopping.If only things had been different I wouldn't have had half the fun,it might have been unusual but you certainly didn't moan.After all I had a coal fire,hot drink and that soggy doughnut to enjoy.

****

"Don't throw caution to the wind"

****

Why could anybody think that the smell of "terry" nappies soaking in a bucket of Milton sanitiser,standing in the corner of the bathroom, or indeed theo dious pungent smell of baby vomit in whichever room I entered,was a good enough reason for me to be excited that I now had a baby brother.It was noisy enough in the house as it was,so the few days of peace I had enjoyed before the homecoming were duly shattered by a non stop wailing and bawling new addition arrived and was quickly whisked upstairs away from me and my sister's toxic presence and thus the pattern was set.Whatever happened from that point was going to be traumatic and consequently it would never really make life comfortable again,Nana,a lady of great perception foresaw his and tried desperately in her final years to attempt to "make things right" but it never really worked.Life to the outside world appeared to be nice and rosy,but the vision broadcast to the world of a happy family
was far from what it appeared to be,with probably what was

considered as having our best interests at heart it was never going to work.

Easter was just around the corner,it was March,but the new baby was all that really mattered,the step children,my sister and I were never going to be accepted as anything more than an inconvenient nuisance to be tolerated..The eleven plus exam results had arrived just before the Easter holidays and I had duly passed,Gosport Grammar School beckoned me with the prospect of joining my current school pals there which would at least soften the blow of leaving my time at Leesland School.

It was customary for the midwife to visit new mothers when they arrived home from Blakes Maternity Hospital during their first days, so it was no surprise when her presence was announced by a knock on the door.I remember that first occasion very well..My sister,who was in her late teens,ran to answer the door and the midwife greeted her saying"how is the new mother,are you and the baby keeping well,"Before she was able to answer she was pushed aside by an hysterical step mother with the words"she's not the mother I am".The bewildered midwife appeared in a state of shock and profoundly apologising entered to a withering stare from the disapproving mother.The pattern was set and the sense of being in the way became ever more apparent,more and more time was spent at Nanas and a visit to Ireland later in the summer of 1961 reinforced what I was already aware of and was to be the pattern for the rest of my childhood.

As the Easter holidays came to an end I prepared myself for my last term at Leesland School,at the end of which after the summer holidays I would join my classmates at the grammar school,or so I thought.All of this was suddenly to change however with the arrival of a long brown envelope which fell through the letterbox addressed to Dad.As he opened it I heard him say"he's got into the grammar school",I couldn't see that it was something we didn't already know,but turning to me he said "well done that's good".Briefly I was puzzled but then it dawned on me, I had taken an entrance exam for another grammar school and perhaps the letter referred to that.When we arrived at Nanas that morning her reaction to the same news seemed less enthusiastic and she was later to tell me why.,perhaps I was correct in my assumption,perhaps it was that other school,Portsmouth Grammar.

Dad drove away with a cursory"bye",having dropped me off on his way to work,leaving Nana to explain to me that my future was to be not at Gosport Grammar but Portsmouth Grammar and none of my school pals would be going there with me.The last term at Leesland School was bittersweet,the school sports,school outing to Carisbrooke Castle in the Isle of Wight and time spent with my friends was great but the lonely prospect of September without those friends, amongst people I had very little in common with was not a thought to relish.

Far too soon the holidays were over, September soon arrived and I was taken one gloomy morning,trembling with trepidation,to the imposing brick barrack building which was Portsmouth Grammar School,a great opportunity I was told, but to me it heralded the start of the worst period of my life,the next seven years were not to be very happy..I was never comfortable there and in 1964 when Nana left this world I was to be on my own,my sister had married,shortly after emigrating to Australia,making home life even less tolerable.

!!!

During the summer holidays,although only about ten or possibly eleven,provided we told Nana where I was going to I would embark on long bicycle rides,starting at Leesland Road and setting off towards Fareham and beyond,really as far as our legs would take us before they became too tired.I would sometimes ride up through Elson where by The Windsor Castle public house there was a small field adjacent to railway crossing with a herd of cattle in it.Along past Elson Church with its magnificent elm tree,then passing Fort Brockhurst with its dark forbidding moat,the water appearing almost black,I would cycle up Fareham Road towards Fareham itself.Up past Holbrook school with its corrugated tin buildings,surrounded by fields with more cows gently browsing and chewing the cud I and my friends would soon approach the naval armament yard at Bedenham.We would wait at the level crossing for a consignment to make its way to the compound which was filled with"bombs",at that time any explosive device be it bomb,depth charge or mine was to me a bomb.In between the various metal casings,incongruously sheep and cattle grazed the grass on which the various armament casings were stored.Continuing on past the factories on the Fareham Road as I approached Tom Parker's Dairies at Cams Alder they had a pedigree herd of dairy cows,that supplied milk daily for the dairy contentedly grazing in the adjacent field.In the field next to them stood the last of the working milk dray ponies,in fact all of the route from Gosport to Fareham had farm animals grazing close to the houses that had started to spring up.There were at the time at least three piggeries in Gosport amongst the houses,one in Clayhall Road,one in Smith Street and one in Elson.

As I rode further into the country there were little fields with neatly cut hedges,well manicured road verges and free flowing ditches with little bridges crossing them,leading to five bar gates which secured their entrances.I would come across cheery farm workers armed with scythes and sickles keeping the vegetation in check,tied to a bike leant up against a nearby tree was an assortment of ditching tools to keep the rainwater running freely.All this laborious working providing much benefit to the wildlife as well as employment for less scholarly individuals.As I continued up towards Boarhunt Church land my companions were lucky enough to see slow worms,adders,harvest mice,even lizards sunning themselves on the tarmac edge of the little used road.Passing the church,partially hidden behind a row of trees we descended down around a sharp left and right bend into the yard of a large farm set around a dirty duck pond.The road ran straight through the centre of the farmyard,ducks and chicken ran amok,on the left a byre of calves,in the field behind it the main herd.Behind the pond on the right were the sheep pens and the storage areas for hay and straw.We would sit by the pond and eat our packed lunches,forced to share them with the various ducks and geese that were attentive companions..Before heading back to tackle the steep hill up past the church on the way home we would go and stroke the calves,with their beautiful large soporific eyes.What a difference half a century makes with all these things no longer available to us or quickly disappearing from the countryside replaced by acres of arable boredom.

****

''Once in a blue moon''

****

Soon after the initial dissent,my sister and I were presented with what we thought was the exciting prospect of a foreign holiday,something few people were as yet lucky enough to experience.We were to go on a visit to Ireland to make the acquaintance of friends of my new "mum" and for dad to visit his old birthplace,Birr in County Offaly,These were the people who for as long as I recall always sent us a small box of withered shamrock to celebrate St. Patrick's Day.The journey was not particularly pleasant,crossing the Irish Sea in a raging storm not to be recommended,in fact in a crowded lounge,rising and falling on a rather dated ferry it was frightening.Little reassured me when I addressed my dad's new wife as mum, to be sharply rebuked by the reply "I am not your mother I'm your auntie"to the amazement of me and our fellow passengers but this was to set the tone of the next few years of my life.The "holiday" was not the most spectacular, the most notable event being the car crash as we returned from Liverpool,and the subsequent steam train ride back to Gosport.As the days went by I was lucky enough to have a haven at Nanas and I took every opportunity to spend my time away from Oxford Road,spending days continuing to play with my friends and entertain myself in relative happiness.By the end of 1958,however,this became harder as one morning we left Oxford Road for school and in the evening returned to a three storey building in Rowner Lane with no garden and just an asphalt roof to play on.I was now living in a two storey maisonette located over I & G Dewane's Wavy Line grocer's shop.Yes they had bought a shop and with it came an even more difficult time of my life.Leesland was still my school so my pals remained the same, nothing much changed,I spent time at Nanas and she ensured,wherever possible, that we had our normal routines.School was interesting and fun,I worked hard,vying with two other pupils,David Reid and Selena Phillips to be top of the class.Throughout primary school the three of us would compete to be top,first,second and third,in no given order at the end of every term.We had moved on now to 1961 and the previous few years had been relatively normal,with only minor changes in daily routines. Dad and his wife pursued their grocery venture and it was proving relatively successful,underpinned by Dad's site agent position,the risk was minimal. had been told that I was to have a new baby brother.or sister in late1960 but when he arrived it just was the beginning of even more upheaval.In March 1961 on a damp misty morning,Dad surprised me by saying we were not going to Leesland School.but instead I was going to Portsmouth to take an examination for a new school,"mum" was in hospital as the baby was due and I felt nervous and not a little bewildered.I had already taken my eleven-plus,so it couldn't be that as we did that at Privet School a few days earlier,consequently I was unsure as to what was to come.The drive to Portsmouth was silent and uneventful,eventually we arrived at an austere barrack style building which we entered via a large white arch similar to the entrance to Haslar Hospital.Inside we entered a high ceilinged room with wooden shutters on the windows and rows of iron framed school desks.I was greeted by a man in a long black gown,wearing a strange square hat, carrying an ominous looking cane under his arm,who pointed me to a seat at one of the desks after asking my name.On the numbered desk was paper and writing materials.Gradually the room filled as more boys arrived,many who apparently knew each other and were dressed in the same school uniform.The clock slowly ticked it's way to nine-thirty precisely at which point we were told to turn the exam papers over which had been placed on each desk."You have two and a half hours" said the man on giving the signal to start and we all turned our papers over,read the questions and started to write feverishly,the man with the cane constantly patrolling the aisles with a menacing glint in his eye.I tried hard not to look up,writing nervously not knowing for once if my answers were right or wrong,I was not sorry to hear the "stop writing" command when it came as the hands on the clock met at twelve o'clock.Papers handed in,outside Dad was waiting,and with a terse"everything o.k." we got into the car and made our way to a small cafe in Southsea for a roast chicken dinner,a rare Treat in itself,more so that it was with Dad.Dinner finished we returned to the school and it's examination room for a second session,before Dad collected me at three o'clock that afternoon to make the return journey home.The journey was punctuated with a few questions as to how the exam had gone,me explaining that I was unsure as the questions were hard and much of it I hadn't learnt about at Leesland School.Approaching Gosport,I was informed that we were not going straight home but visiting Blakes Maternity Hospital in Elson as Dad was going to see my new baby half brother! The car park at the tiny maternity hospital was dimly lit by rather weak street lamps,the surrounding bushes moved in the wind creating shadows and making loud groaning noises.Children,were not welcome in maternity hospitals,strangely enough,not exactly welcome at any hospitals in fact,so locked in a dark car,frightened of the dark,cold and cowering in my seat the next hour was not the most pleasant, comfortable or inspiring.Eventually a dark figure appeared,it was Dad,who began to extol the qualities of my new baby brother,presumably at that age better than mine,as we travelled home.That was the start,from that day everything changed and very little of it was going to enhance my future home life.

****

''You can't make an omelette without breaking eggs''

****

It was cold,there was no snow,wintery days had been with us for a while,today was the day before Christmas Eve and the excitement was reaching fever pitch.At Mr Jones,the butchers on the corner of Vernon Road the chickens were hanging,some still with feathers,their beady eyes under the red cockscombs lifelessly staring at the ceiling,from a rail at the back of the counter and down both sides of the door frame as you entered the shop.I sidled in,careful not to get drips of blood on my clothes.Once inside what seemed to me to be whole cows hung alongside pigs and sheep waiting to be portioned for the Christmas customers.The red and chrome mincer churned out pork sausage meat,the butcher's boy constantly feeding it,the following day he would be on the delivery bike non stop from dawn to dusk.A pigs head and large greyish ox tongues were stacked on the marble slabs of the display counters,waiting to be purchased in exchange for the little white card filled with pink stamps,the Christmas Club card which had been added to weekly so there was enough money at this time of year.Christmas was not a last minute event ,it had to be saved for all year,even if the actual purchasing was in only a few days prior to the event.All through the night of December 23rd the butcher was at his block,rolls of beef,legs of pork,chickens all readied to ensure everything was on the table Christmas Day.Preparations gathered pace,Christmas Eve was for the final chance,after then you went without,except for milk and cream which was delivered,fresh,soon after midnight on Christmas Day,The milkman was not the only one to deliver to the door on the day,the postman struggled from door to door,laden down,ensuring that even on Christmas Day everyone would get their greetings cards delivered on time.Boxing Day tips were more important then the extra effort that had been put in was felt to deserve a reward however small.

****

''I see said the blind man''

****

When the visit to the lady behind the counter in the post office was over,Dad and I returned to the car and I sat waiting inside whilst Dad visited the John Hunt's site office to check on the progress of his builders.At the time the SETT,diving,tower had just been completed and he was very pleased that he had worked on such an important and advanced facility.Sitting quietly in the car,the promise of an ice cream enough to have me on best behaviour,I watched the to-ing and fro-ing of the nurses and doctors punctuated by the odd arrival of a navy blue

ambulance decorated by a large red cross in the centre of a round white decal.Eventually dad returned from the builders wooden site hut,he said nothing,which was not unusual,started the engine,and drove towards the arched exit,no seat belt required,no seat belt in cars of that era.At the exit he stopped to have his permit checked by the inevitable armed naval rating who was backed up by the military police sat in the red brick office.Turning right we passed the entrance to HMS Dolphin,where I excitedly peered through the gates to catch a glimpse of the many submarines moored inside, befcre turning right along the road which ran along the top of the sloping stone block sea wall.As we drove along,peering at the various ships navigating the choppy,murky, grey-green sea,coasters,tugs,ferries and larger vessels,oil tankers,liners and warships,I remember the nerves,hoping that Dad would not go too close to the edge,particularly if a car or lorry was viewed coming in the opposite direction on the narrow road.Having travelled the length of the wall we headed inland back along Clayhall Road,passing Bailey's piggeries and Haslar Naval cemetery before turning once more towards the seafront at the National Children's Home,and then right along the road to Stoke's Bay.The large houses with long front gardens,overlooking the Solent,seemed to me like

mansions and dad pointed one out as being owned by Mr Pat Hunt,one of his bosses.We then turned up Jellicoe Avenue,passed the waterworks,The Wiltshire Lamb,Harvest Home and War Memorial Hospital before returning to Nana's house in Leesland Road where I went in.Having exchanged a few words with Nana and Grandad he left to return to work,saying he would see me at home that evening.It was some months later before I saw the lady again,but on this occasion Dad had taken me out for tea in a bungalow in Walton Road,off of Gordon Road,a little road just south of Leesland School.I walked shyly into the bungalow,slightly afraid of the new unfamiliar surroundings,to be given an indifferent,lukewarm welcome,almost as if I was an intrusion.I remember the photographs on the sideboard,three in total,one of a bespectacled man,one of the lady with another man,and the third was of an older couple.Who the people were I didn't know and I was no wiser when I left,having enjoyed some home made cake and orange squash,the one good thing about the entire afternoon.Dad was a man of few words when home and a terse exchange with Nana on arrival home seemed to be slightly ominous.I recall the phrase "just promise me the children will be o.k."being uttered by Nana as Dad left.There were no more such events,although there seemed to be a rather awkward atmosphere whenever Dad and Nana met, until one morning in 1957.My sister and I were getting washed and dressed ready for school,finally we were sat in front of the old beige tiled fireplace,waiting for Nana to arrive to walk us to school.Suddenly dad entered the room as normal to say "goodbye" as he was leaving to go to work.Turning away,he paused in the doorway and said,"oh by the way I'm getting married today",then walked out, that evening when we returned home it was to a completely different house,with a new "mother".Wrong footed,unable to understand fully what was taking place,I reacted in my anger and frustration resulting in n act of impetuosity on my part ending with me launching the fire poker through the window!

****

"Empty vessels make most sound"

****

Christmas was such an exciting time in 1954,it was a happy time then for children,certainly not a lot of presents, but the Christmas tree,carol singers,decorations and "luxury food"made it so very special.It was a time for families to celebrate,many who were making up for the disruption of the wartime years,this year however had witnessed a sad event for us at home,the events of October had caste a heavy shadow over our normal celebrations .Nobody felt like partying,the Milk Tray,Quality Street,sugared almonds,sugar mice, chocolate brazils, chocolates,cakes,roast dinner,mince pies,Christmas pudding and trifle had all seemed to have lost their flavour,after all Mum was missing,never to return.I could feel the palpable sadness,the decorations were less shiny,we ate our meals in a mood of almost delayed shock and although friends and neighbours rallied around it wasn't to be the same.Presents,however elaborate,however many,however welcome, couldn't replace Mum.1955 was the year that saw the start of changes in my life that would eventually at a later Christmas bring me to a festive newsagents in Rowner Road,with a man,who dementia apart,had really never been the father I would have liked..One day in 1955 I remember him ollecting me from Nanas,in the school holiday and taking me to his work for a treat,a treat indeed as my life was distanced from him as since Mum died,he never seemed to be around,not his fault as I think he found it difficult to master his grief and the responsibility of two young children.I remember proudly sitting in the front seat of the pale blue and white Hillman Minx as we made our way along the tree lined streets,Whitworth,Gordon,Bury and Foster Roads,all of them with a touch of almost rurality as the fresh green shoots sprung into life from the lime trees.Approaching St Mary's Church in Alverstoke we passed by the children's home and proceeded along Clayhall Road,passing the Gilkicker mile mark,the Naval Cemetery and Bailey's pig sties,to call it a farm would have been too presumptuous.The road followed along a high wall,behind which stood Haslar Naval Hospital,before it turned right towards H M S Dolphin and Haslar Sea Wall.Half way along the road on the right was a white stone pillared archway marking the entrance to the imposing edifice that stood behind the hiding wall.I remember the car turning into the entrance which opened out into a huge parade ground and being stopped by a naval guard,who to my awe and amazement had a real gun,the most memorable fact being that Dad said it was loaded!..I retreated into the car seat on my best behaviour,not wishing to be shot,the guard peered in,checked Dad's security pass and waved us on.The area in front of us had various flower beds dotted around its edges,patriotically planted with red salvia,white alyssum and blue

112

lobelia, around the perimeter were cars parked facing the buildings walls.An archway leading through the barrack like building also provided access to the accommodation and wards within it.As we entered I can recall nurses with neat starched white uniforms,some in dark blue with white wimples and red belts,white coated doctors with shiny chrome stethoscopes hanging round their necks,and orderlies in white pushing heavy cream coloured cast iron bedsteads between wards.I walked silently along a high ceilinged corridor with glass paned doors leading to the wards running off both sides,it smelt of Tcp and disinfectant and at the end led to a high dark wooden door through which we entered.Little children were seen and not heard,Dad was a rigid disciplinarian,so I walked closely by his side as we crossed the room to a high counter which had a wire screen above it,a gap at the bottom being enough to slip letters under.This was Haslar Post Office and after being told to say "hello" to the lady behind the counter I was sat on a stool,told to be quiet and wait,until Dad was ready to take me home.This was the first time I met the person who was to eventually enter my life as a replacement for my Mum,a day I recall with a certain fear and the start of the side of my life's experiences that I came to dislike the most.

****

''A bad workman always blames his tools''

****

It was a Wednesday afternoon in December 2002,it was the time of year for buying presents.Two men,one elderly and needing help as he shuffled along,walking stick in hand,whilst the younger man carried a wire shopping basket which was being loaded with various boxes of chocolates.The older man had wanted to buy Christmas gifts for people he knew and the two of them had driven to the newsagents in Rowner Road situated in the parade of shops at the top of Masten Crescent.As they shopped another man of similarly advanced years approached the older man."Hello Gerry thought you were dead,haven't seen you for so long"he said.The addressed man turned with a vacant bewildered look,his lack of recognition betraying his mental condition."He doesn't come out very often,but he wanted to get a few Christmas gifts,so I brought him around in the car" said the younger man and the person who had spoken turned,"and who are you?"he asked."I'm his son" said the younger man,a reply greeted with "he's only got one son and a daughter"."No" replied the younger man,"he has two son's"."Well I've known him for thirty years and he's never said he had another son ".I can assure you said the younger man that this is my father.The two older men,now aware of who each other were,discussed albeit it rather disjointedly,the people they had known and were no longer alive.Eventually the ghosts were put to rest and the conversation concluded,they wished one another Happy Christmas and the younger man and his elderly companion approached the checkout point to pay for their purchases,having added a couple of bottles of festive spirit to complete the basket of presents.On returning,in silence,to the old man's bungalow in Masten Crescent the son helped the father from the car and carried in the shopping,much to the amusement of the woman who was waiting inside with a welcome cup of tea.We only bought what was on his list was the only comment I made.Tea drunk,goodbyes said,the younger man clambered back into the car to make the forty mile drive home.He had plenty of time on the journey home to reflect on how we had arrived in this situation but the solution was now too late.How could outwardly people be so different to how you knew them,why could the signs have been missed.Perhaps they weren't,perhaps it was the result of what was acceptable in the the past,perhaps that event in 1954,when Mum had died, began the chapter of memories which were to result over a period of many years in me being forgotten.

****

"You must make hay whilst the sun shines"

****

Standing at the front door,the snow was falling once more,soft flakes drifted and floated as they swirled around in the soft glow of the gas lamp.The single deck number 6 Provincial bus crept cautiously along the snow covered road and was slowly coming to a halt at the bus stop, at the end of Norman Road, sliding uncontrollably into the kerbside gutter.I climbed on board,my feet slipping on the step,the soles of my shoes caked with hard packed snow.I had hardly seated myself before the almost empty bus pulled away,its wheels spinning to get a grip,three men,passing by on their way home from work,stepped out behind to help shove it on its way.As the wheels gripped and it lurched forward the men almost slipped over as the impetus with them leaning forward left them with no grip on the icy surface.The yellow headlights picked out the wayward snowflakes as they fell,its slow ineffective wiper struggling to clear the snow which was building up on the windscreen, the driver wide eyed stared ahead looking for obstacles.As it passed Nana standing at the door he waved his hand in greeting and starting to shiver I retreated further down the bus.The following Monday I would return to school and we would exchange experiences of the snow and Christmas just gone,excitedly talking of our presents and what adventures had taken place.Later in the week the snowfall saw the cancellation of the bus service,so I had to spend the night at Leesland Road,unable to walk on the icy pavements,

****

''All that glitters is not gold''

****

Making my way downstairs,the snow had been falling all night,it seemed less inviting when I stayed at Nanas than at home,primarily due to the prospect of the toilet arrangements being outside.The layer of snow with the odd paw print where a cat had passed earlier seemed less exciting than it had been the night before,as did the journey to the outside "privy" which would probably be frozen solid when I arrived there.The water in the toilet bowl had already turned to ice and the solid ice block which had formed in the iron cistern meant you couldn't flush the toilet when you had used it,at that point you just wished you had been the first one there that morning.Nana had already made up the coal fire,it was thankfully reducing the chill inside,the fire ashes from the previous night having been placed in a zinc pail and taken to be sprinkled over the intended path to the "wee outhouse".Having braved the chill wind blowing up the backyard,accompanying the snow, it was no holiday when eventually sitting my warm bottom on the freezing wooden seat,my fingers freezing and teeth chattering,to be followed by the luxury of newspaper squares,printers ink and the frozen cistern.When finished I couldn't even hurry back indoors without the risk of the now only slightly warm bottom getting even colder with sharp contact on the frozen ground as the ashes failed to perform their required purpose.

"There's no point in flogging a dead horse"

Today,was Saturday and there was one last treat associated with Christmas before the holiday ended.Today was the day of the children's party, organised by Dad's employers,John Hunts,which took place at the school hall of Bridgemary School.The morning seemed to last forever and passing time by playing with one or two of the presents from Christmas Day only slightly sped it up.As the clock approached three o'clock I sat dressed in my best clothes,which were almost identical to the ones I wore everyday,my hair was parted to one side and I was already to go.Away we went.I climbed into Dad's car and we slowly slid our way over the slippery roads on the journey from Leesland Road to Bridgemary School.On arrival,as we entered the building we were encouraged to remove our slush laden shoes,so as not to dirty the floor.Having done so and hung our coats on the hooks supplied we were greeted in the hall by groaning tables,full of party food, sandwiches,jelly,blancmange and fancy cakes.A tall Christmas tree twinkled merrily in one corner and what looked like hundreds of balloons,filled a net which was hanging from the ceiling..All morning John Hunt's employees had been decorating the hall to welcome the now arriving noisy rabble of children of various ages.We excitedly ran,shouted,screamed and slid on the polished wooden floor of the hall until we were at last sat down at long tables for tea.The small triangular sandwiches,cakes and my lasting memory of red jelly set in little square waxed cardboard "bowls" were soon devoured,the occasional jelly being used as a missile.Having eaten,the floor swept, we sat in front of the stage whilst a simple,conjurer,magician or ventriloquist entertained us,there was always one child who would spoil the magic."I know how you did it,you put it in your pocket" would come a shout from the back row,the entertainment followed by party games,musical chairs or pin the tail on the donkey.'The show over,the entertainer certainly exhausted,even though the children still had energy in abundance,games finished, it was time for Father Christmas to arrive.The double door at the rear of the hall swung open to reveal Father Christmas,who entered complete with red sack and made his way to the pile of presents stacked close to the tree.Each of us was called up in turn,"given a kind word" then presented with an unknown present,blue wrapping paper for boys,red wrapping paper for girls.Everything was going well until a little boy yelled out,expelling the myth with,"your not Father Christmas your Tommy's dad".Tears from some smaller children ensued,but they were soon replaced by laughter as the release of the net of balloons, meant frantic chasing of them followed by numerous pops and bangs.Clutching my present in one hand,a highly prized balloon in the other I,with the other children was reunited with a parent, who would appear to reluctantly claim their wayward child, it was all over for another year.Simple,great fun and always looked forward to,my present cheap,but to me as priceless as gold.

****
.

"You mustn't let the cat out of the bag"

****

It was over,all the hard work and thrift of the last twelve months had at last achieved its aim.The coppers,sixpences,bobs,florins,threepenny bits,farthings and half crowns saved steadfastly all year had been counted and were ready to spend to augment the home made provisions already lovingly prepared in the kitchen.It was the final days before the true reason for the celebration of Christmas,not presents and food but the birth of Jesus in Bethlehem many centuries before.It had been,busy,exciting and for me impatient waiting for the day to come and I must admit the present was an attractive thought amongst the other pertinent reasons.."As God imparted to human hearts" we sang carols on the street going to school,at school and in that important of all houses,St Faith's Church in Tribe Road.As the worshippers filed from the church after celebrating midnight mass,Father Christmas frantically criss-crossed the sky with his reindeer and sleigh to deliver to all "good little children" before they awoke..We quickly hid under the bedclothes,anxious not to be seen, in

case by doing so,Father Christmas passed me by.Several times I started to venture downstairs,only to be deterred by the noise of an adult who would possibly intercept us.Eventually I could wait no longer,summoning all my courage I ventured forth,crept downstairs and stealthily emptied my stocking,which hung from the mantlepiece.I had devoured the penny chocolate bar before breakfast,and was looking forward to the apple,orange,banana and nuts in shell which nestled in the toe of the stocking.

****

"You must go to any port in a storm"

****

The homemade pickles,chutneys and pickled onions all stood on the festive table,at suppertime accompaniment for the cheddar cheese and cold meats,tongue,beef,ham,gammon and chicken which filled the platters alongside the crusty bread and golden yellow butter,all taking their part in the celebration.Paynes sugared almonds and chocolate brazil nuts,Callard and Bowsers nougat,Quality Street assortment and Politi's Turkish delight had been emptied from the pressed vaseline glass bowls on the top of the sideboard which were washed then put away till the same time next year.I had enjoyed playing with the colourful balloons,so difficult to inflate,so easy to let down,my cousins popped them just to see me cry I,had wound my clockwork train endlessly,I had laughed and cried and that slight dusting of snow on Boxing Day had put a twinkle in my eye.Christmas would come again but not till next year,never exactly the same,the finality would sink home in five days as the decorations were stored away on "twelfth night",it was unlucky to keep them hanging any longer.It wouldn't be long though before small yellow downy chicks would occupy the chicken run at the bottom of the garden again and so the process begin once more.

****

"Time and tide wait for no man"

'**

The last dying seconds ticked away,as the old year died a new one began,I had experienced "Auld Lang Syne" sung with gusto as the old year died and the new one was now born,I had waited with baited breath for "the tall dark stranger bearing coal" to cross the doorstep to bring us luck,"first footing" was an ancient tradition.I had had it all,Christmas had been wondrous,even the simplest things seemed like luxuries,I was grateful for the smallest of gifts.I enjoyed all I had been gifted however cheap,it was the thought that counted not the cost.Simple toys,often of wood,made by Grandad in the garden shed,a train,a lorry,soap box or toy castle,on one occasion a set of painted wooden soldiers.Very little money,but the effort put into the toys was well worth it on Christmas Morning,cost was not important,the value came in the surprise,no lists of what I wanted,I had what I was given and I was grateful,never disappointed,only proud of what I had received. Another year had begun,what it would bring I knew not, but what it did bring I would make the most of,there would be good and bad,sorrow and joy but most important of all the end would be the same provided there were no major upsets.

"A Happy Christmas"

****

"Let it live to fight another day"

****

The afternoon sky was relatively blue,if a little pale,small white cirrus clouds floated slowly,almost imperceptibly across the vast expanse of space,it was only dinner time but you could feel winter in the air,as it started to become colder.Snow had threatened earlier in the week but had now receded,in the little garden next door a small fire of damp leaves and applewood sent small swirls of sweet selling smoke into the still air,the final tidy up in the garden now completed. Nana and I,smartly dressed with thick scarves and gloves,were ready to combat the low temperature which was only going to become lower as we set off from 80 Leesland Road,on our way to my uncle's New Years Eve party.It was a long walk on a cold day,buses didn't run on New Years Eve ,very few working class people had cars and taxis were expensive and had to be prebooked.Taxis,themselves,weren't numerous and we had booked one for the return journey when it would be dark and street lights were not terribly effective so to have one now was just too extravagant.We set off at a sprightly pace,not only because it was a long way,it was also helpful in keeping warm.Through Tribe Road,then Harcourt Road, down Whitworth and Gordon Road before joining the more rural Green Lane.The mature trees looked like skeletons against the sky,the remnants of the autumn leaf litter lay on the muddy,stony path,disguising the odd puddle.At the end of Green Lane we skirted past Alverstoke junior school and crossed over to enter the often flooded road which bordered Alver Creek opposite St Mary's Church.The tide was ebbing,going out,and as it did left seaweed,grass and the odd small crab along the high tide line which ran along the line of the tidal road.At the end before it turned towards Gosport Park a right turn took us up onto the old Stokes Bay railway line,over Alver Bridge,long disused,now just a shingle track which after a short walk arrived at Clayhall Road.Taking this road which skirted the end of Alver Creek,with its mudflats springing sea lavender,sea thrift and samphire,it led us to The Haven,a small unadopted cul de sac surfaced with gravel,situated opposite a little grocers shop,our destination being number four at the very end.We entered through a wooden gate,down a concrete path and up two steps to the front door where my uncle,aunt and cousins were already there to greet us.My aunts mum.Mrs Merritt and other family members were also there as they lived just along the road at number one. Almost immediately we arrived the games commenced,Postman's Knock,Pin the tail on the Donkey,Blind Man's Bluff and Musical Chairs were all enjoyed,alcohol flowed and an air of merriment soon availed.There was much laughter,many tears and the odd squabble and accusation of cheating but it always ended happily and with a sumptuous tea.The usual items of rabbits or castles moulded from red jelly or pink blancmange,a huge bowl of trifle,various sandwiches,iced cakes,mince pies and Cadbury's chocolate finger biscuits loaded the table and in a very short space of time it was well depleted,my favourite being the Cadbury's chocolate fingers.Once the table had been cleared away,the washing up finished, we all sat around the table,glasses charged with various drinks,paper party hats from the crackers,worn at various jaunty angles the next round of entertainment about to commence.By now alcohol was playing a large part in the activities,items were dropped and fumbled,at one point during a game of "Pass the Parcel"layers of paper were being added rather than removed.Card games,ludo and hoopla would pass the time between tea and supper as the television remained switched off,the only time it was on was for the queen's speech or possibly the afternoon film.However you can only watch "Sink the Bismarck"or"The Battle of the River Plate" so many times! Soon after,seemingly only minutes,we had eaten tea,the table was laid once more,an impressive supper of cold meat, cheese and pickles was served, most of us not having had time to recover from the first offering.

****

"You shouldn't hide your light under a bushel"

****

At ten thirty,on the dot,a pre-booked taxi would arrive to take Nana and myself home,except on this occasion I was being allowed to stay later as long as I arrived home by one o'clock. I thought this was a great idea,as I was only thirteen at the time I jumped at the chance to stay later my oversight being that I was frightened of the dark.My excitement had obscured my mind to the fact that it was cold,dark and that I would be on my own.It was about forty five minutes to an hour at a steady jog to get back to Leesland Road so once midnight had passed and New Year greetings exchanged, I left The Haven the bright moon and twinkling stars having become obscured by the large ominous clouds drifting across the sky.I had barely reached Alver Creek,its dark water looking particularly uninviting when the first flakes began to fall,my nervous jog increased in pace and so did the snow,having ran down Clayhall Road and nervously past St Mary's churchyard I entered the dark shadows in Green Lane,but with its well spaced lamps it seemed quite welcoming.Ineffective at the best of times they threw little light on the tree lined path,every shadow,every rustle saw my nervous fear increase.its welcome overestimated The snow by now was deep enough to show my footsteps and I could feel my feet beginning to slip.I tried to run faster,shying away from the shadows but things were to get even worse.As I entered Gordon Road the street lamps started to go out,in the fifties and early sixties they didn;t stay on all night,unless they were one of the few gas lamps still in use.Suddenly the trees which lined the road became scary figures,I imagined all manner of things,my feet were slipping as I ran,the faster I ran the more they slipped,as I glanced around to ensure nobody was following me,almost in a hysterical panic to get home,it happened.My path was not entirely straight as I ran and I caught the side of the odd tree,but as I brushed this particular one there was a soft thud and a mumbling sound as I passed,the tree I had just brushed against had been the crutch of some poor inebriate leaning against it.I couldn't stop I was running now at world record pace by the time I entered Harcourt Road I was travelling faster than anyone had ever run.Tribe Road was a blur and pulling up at number 80, I pushed up the sash window,took the key from the window cill and desperately opened the front door,panting in panic,Nana's voice rang out "is that you"."Yes", I replied nonchalantly,who else she thought it might be at that time of night I have no idea "it's snowing quite hard now you know it took longer than I thought to get home." That night was the start of one of the worst winters I have ever known,it was January 1963.I just hope the person I had felled on Gordon Road woke up before the snow covered them,but I feel sure I would have heard if they hadn't.

****

"Least said,soonest mended"

****

With Boxing day over,there seemed little to look forward to,we didn't really celebrate New Year's Day unless I went with Nana to my uncles,at home nothing happened as dad disapproved of alcohol,other than sherry in the trifle apart from "first footing" at the neighbours it was a non event..There were certainly no fireworks and it was normally the adults who had a New Year drink with a raucous rendering of "Auld Lang Syne" to welcome the new year in.Apart from this brief interlude the only other possible excitement on the horizon was my return to school a few days later,the next festival of note Shrove Tuesday or aster itself.The Christmas leftovers,there was so much food that it mustn't be wasted,still had to be eaten,we didn't even have any chickens to feed now so this was where the housewives came into their own.Many had seen"service", or had been members of the Women's Institute,their ingenuity knew no limits,at a time when nothing was to be wasted.Everything needed to be eaten,there were no fridges,so dishes using cold meat and bubble and squeak making use of surplus cooked vegetables were very prominent in most resourceful households,stews,pies and puddings.Dad had leftovers,savoury or sweet, in his lunchbox for what seemed forever,lemonade and beer bottles mounted up waiting to be taken to the "offie" to claim the cash deposits paid when they had been purchased.Nothing was wantonly wasted,what wasn't eaten because of it being"on the turn" still didn't get wasted as the pigman would collect it to add to the pig swill.Christmas pudding,sometimes ended up fried,mince pies,with their added brandy lasted forever.The Christmas cake with its icing getting harder by the day adorned the tea table for some time,although the marzipan,or almond paste was still quite agreeable.One year a maroon trike,another year a blue pedal car,very basic with no ostentatious embellishments,even a pair of stilts occupied the days between Christmas and the resumption of school.Any money received at Christmas could be turned into Airfix model kits,packets of beads for the girls and "painting by number" oil painting sets or rubber plaster of paris moulds for making ornaments.On occasions,most years, my wish for snow was fulfilled as the weather seemed to change after Christmas, with frosts and winds increasing as they blew from the north and sometimes there was enough snow for me to build a snowman."A favourite saying of Nanas was "when the north wind doth blow then we shall have snow and what will poor robin do then poor thing,poor thing".Along the terrace of houses every garden was home to a snowman,even adults joined in,throwing a sly snowball at the neighbour as they ventured out,blaming some unsuspecting child I would see how far I could throw one, trying to hit my pals who lived three doors down,more often than not missing the target,occasionally the wayward projectile genuinely hitting an unsuspecting neighbour.Every snowman was smartly dressed with an old scarf wrapped around his neck,in some cases not so old,they had a hat placed on top of an icy head with nose and eyes made of small pieces

126

of coal,further coal was used to make the buttons on his imaginary coat,finally sticks or pieces of twig were added to give him,or her. arms.Amongst all of this the solitary figure of a little red breasted robin,its feathers fluffed up,hid in the lee of a sheltering tree to keep out of the wind.

****

"Mind your p's and q's"

****

As the days passed we would have presented to us the prospect of John Hunt's Christmas Childrens party,every company seemed to have
one for the employees children,and of course there was the perennial
family pantomime,attended quite often after school had reconvened on
a January weekend.I was lucky, I remember the journey which led us to the King's Theatre in Southsea where the performance was enjoyed,normally it took place on a Saturday afternoon.We made the journey in Dad's Ford Prefect,"a sit up and beg" draughty,poorly heated car,the wind blew through the ill fitting windows and doors,rain filtered in through cracks and crevices and we were so glad to arrive and get out.Dad parked the car around the corner from the theatre,then we briskly walked back to join the already growing queue waiting to get into the auditorium,under an ornate glass canopy,At last we were in the foyer and crossed to the little window where we collected the pre-booked tickets.Usherettes,with little tiara like headbands,would stand selling Kia-ora orange drink cartons from a tray suspended around their neck.Salted peanuts were dispensed into little paper bags from a glass machine,suitably inscribed,salty,warm

and greasy with a distinctive nutty smell..Monkey nuts,in their little brown husks were also available,these were unroasted peanuts in shells,for those who preferred to "shuck" their own,or weren't keen on salt.The velour seats were extremely uncomfortable but as I spent most of the time standing up it didn't really matter.I waited with excitement for the Ugly Sisters to throw us sweets,our outstretched hands eager to catch them,I laughed at the slapstick,custard pies and water which the clowning characters liberally spread around and I watched bewildered as "famous people",I had never heard of, performed enthusiastically.I remember at various pantomimes,Joe Brown and the Bruvvers,Bert Wheedon,Keith Harris with Orville,Harry H Corbett with Sooty,Sweep and Sue,Pinky and Percy,all the stars of the day,and what fabulous days of fun and laughter they were.

****

Nothings impossible if you put your mind to it"

****

Eventually,looking slightly paler,the table was set up for tea and the party food began to appear.A large meat plate with a cooked ham,another with the ever present home cooked Ox tongue,were joined by sliced corned beef and a small dish containing tinned luxury red salmon,the rest of the year it would the pink variety if you could afford it at all.An enormous recycled sweet jar of home pickled onions,jars of various pickle,home made chutney,pickled red cabbage,pickled beetroot and the inevitable pickled walnuts.As the table groaned,tinned Heinz potato and vegetable salad,similar to chunky sandwich spread,appeared,a wooden breadboard crowned with a large uncut loaf accompanied by butter and cheese dishes took its place,then the previously mentioned carving knife,now washed,accompanied by a two pronged carving fork was placed ready for use.As I juggled one handed to carry items to the already straining table the little room became ever more crowded,aunts,uncles,cousins and second cousins,everyone turned up at Nana's Boxing Day party.Having said hello to Grandad,who through all this was still resolutely sat glued to his armchair,accompanied by his bottle of stout and saying very little,they all retreated to the front room which contained the Christmas tree,to await the invitation to sit at the table.Eventually everyone had arrived and they were summoned to the festive table,Uncle Dennis,Auntie Verna,myself,sister Valerie,cousins ony,Graham and Melvin,Nana,Grandad,but never Dad,why I never knew.The next few hours were to make the incident with the carving knife pale into insignificance,up and down the country many families would be celebrating in the same way,but our chaotic scenes were unlikely to have been bettered,but then with so many people in such a small terraced house it was possibly to have been expected.

It all started well enough,eating our way through the piles of food,until my cousins and sister decided to play a trick on me,as if they hadn't caused me enough suffering already.They were aware that I was very partial to pickled onions,even at a young age,anything tasting vinegary I loved so they persuaded me into taking the largest onion from the jar and put it into my mouth ....whole!! Not wishing to be seen as a whimp or coward,thinking it funny I played ball,as you can imagine the result of having a large vinegary pickled onion,which I couldn't chew,firmly wedged in my mouth had spectacular results.My face became redder and redder making my blood from an earlier event seem comparatively pale.Unable to turn the onion in my mouth and the acid vinegar taking its toll the tears started pouring from my eyes as I became hotter and hotter and breathing became more and more difficult..As I choked certain individuals,also in tears,from laughing,laughed even louder as I was severely reprimanded by Nana for doing something so silly.My ordeal ended at last and the remains of the meal were cleared away,the pass the parcel ended in more tears as I never won the prize due to being distracted when it was my turn to unwrap a layer of paper,but there was to be a lull and a little respite as my antagonists decided to target poor old Grandad,who never did any harm.At Christmas there was always a box of indoor "fireworks",to be lit at sometime during the evening,which apart from the tiny sparklers were less fire,more smoke,the acrid smoke from one smelt particularly awful.There was one like a military tank which expelled acrid smoke accompanied by the odd red glow, another of Churchill smoking a dubious smelling cigar,a small tablet which when lit provided "snow" and the "piece de resistance" which grandad was about to experience as he did every year.Well fed and watered Grandad had been sat dozing from the effects of his bottles of stout,roll up cigarette in hand,as he roused,taking a glance around, he lit his"smoke"as he called it,two puffs,then a third,the assembled throng waited with bated breath.Four,five and on the sixth puff it exploded,the little "banger" inserted into his cigarette had exploded as expected by everyone except for Grandad.How he never had a heart attack I will never know,a hasty retreat by the laughing teenagers into the front room came none too soon as he spluttered and cursed.My cousins and sister, being older than me,thought that I was a source of entertainment for them,so once in the front room they thought it would be fun,for them,to get me to go outside onto the pavement.Pretending they had dropped the front door key outside,when in fact they threw it out, they persuaded me that so they wouldn't get into trouble, that I should climb past the Christmas tree,out of the sash window, onto the pavement to retrieve it. Being no more than eight,I readily obliged to get in their good books,"be one of them '.They however had a different idea so it shouldn't have come as a surprise that having retrieved the key the window had been closed.I was now stood outside,unable to get in the window,too short to reach the keyhole in the door to open it,even though I had the key,cold and crying I started to bang on the door to get back in,the adults heard the commotion and came to see what it was.Opening the door with"what are you doing out there" I briefly explained at which my uncle knocked on the front room door saying"let him join in he can't do any harm",but that was to be their downfall,and almost all our downfalls.Once outside they had started to light the red candles on the Christmas tree against the wishes of Nana who had told them that they weren't to do it.Attracted by my banging on the door, as the grown ups came to see what was going on,their frantic efforts to extinguish the lit candles,led to one candle falling,resulting in the tree catching fire.Chaos ensued as they fled the room to escape the now burning tree,as the adults tried to enter it,eventually doing so and smothering the flames before the situation became totally irretrievable..I never understand however,why it turned out,once again to be my fault that the problem had transpired in the first place.

****

"All good things come to an end,nothing lasts forever"

****

All children loved Christmas,just as they do now,but it wasn't quite the same,unlike in later years, we had to make do with many things,replacing or renewing was out of the question,limited by the availability of spare money.Only if it was irreparable was it thrown away and a new or secondhand replacement sourced.So with this in mind I looked at my 1950's Christmas from a different angle looking at what we reused.There were items which even we today reuse but from memory there were some,what now would be cheap throwaway items that went on forever.From pickle to pudding we reused the same items year after year,the normal items Kilner jars,jamjars,white china pudding basins,the washed out linen pudding clothes,mostly used throughout the year,Christmas being no different.There was however items that would probably surprise many,not so old folk,that were kept from year to year including wrapping paper. The Christmas cake had shiny silver dragees and shiny royal icing,but the frill around the sides,the little chalk figures of the snowman,the toboggan,Father Christmasand the christmas tree,even the foil paper Happy Christmas were all the donations from previous years cakes.The crepe paper garlands,the paper lanterns that were hung from the ceiling,all became objects of celebration as they lasted another year with no further expense.The decorations on the tree,glass baubles,small crackers,the red wax candles,the clip on holders,even the cotton wool that pretended to be snow.At the extreme the Christmas Tree was dug up from the garden and replanted every year once it had performed its duty.Seasonal items like festive crockery and glass bowls came out just at Christmas but one item stuck in my memory more than most and that surrounded the pudding.It was a tradition to have silver sixpences,once it had been silver threepenny coins,wrapped in greaseproof paper,placed in the rich fruit Christmas pudding before it was cooked.Whoever had the slice of pudding with the coin in was said to enjoy wealth in the following year,however silver sixpences were becoming scarce so the coin was exchanged for a modern substitute,the silver sixpence stored for the next years pudding.

****

''Your making a mountain out of a molehill''

I snugly cradled the hot water bottle,gazing through sleep laden eyes and a whispered "do I have to go to bed,it's too early to go to bed'.Although it was only nine o'clock,it was way past my normal bedtime,the excitement of the day had caught up with me so I reluctantly made my way up ''the wooden hill''. Accompanied by Nana with an enamel candlestick to illuminate the way,I knelt to hurriedly say my prayers,removed my dressing gown,climbed into a chilly bed and having been duly "tucked in" I quickly drifted off to the "land of nod" to dream of tomorrow and more excitement.Boxing Day dawned bright and cold,sunny but certainly not warm,I had seen the ice patterns on the draughty windows,staying warm in bed a little longer seemed a better option than shivering downstairs,although I desperately wanted to be out riding my new trike.By the time I had crept downstairs for breakfast the scullery was a hive of industry,Nana never seemed to sleep and today was no exception,lunch would be cold meat and bubble and squeak,minimum preparation,as all effort was directed towards preparing for the family party,taking place that afternoon and evening.The gas stove was already struggling under the weight of heavy pots,one contained a large gammon joint,whilst others contained boiling water and milk.Moulds lay upturned awaiting their blancmange and jelly,in one corner a ready set jelly containing sponge cake,tinned fruit cocktail and a smidgin of sherry was waiting in a large glass bowl for its layer of home made custard which once set and cooled would be covered with some type of cream,often from a tin,then finally sprinkled with sugar strands and silver dragees to make a delicious,"adult only'' trifle.The ox tongue,cooked and skinned the previous day,before being pressed under a wooden breadboard with a brick on top,now sat resplendent on a meat plate,alongside it a wedge shaped cheese dish and a bowl of Heinz potato or vegetable salad from a tin.There was no salad dressings,salad cream was not around and you purchased olive oil from the chemist to put warm into your ear"to soften the wax",not to use for a salad dressing.Fresh salad was itself,a scarce product as it was out of season and maybe an imported tomato or two would be all you could buy.The morning passed quickly,I rode my trike up and down the pavement excitedly ringing the bell at nothing,stopping frequently to check that the box on the back was still empty,sometimes complemented by a passer by.Dinner time,the meal consisting of cold meat,pickles and bubble and squeak,curtailed any further riding,so the bike was put in the shed,As soon as dinner was cleared away I was sent off to get ready for the party,the tables being positioned by the adults,then I had to sit and wait,"I mustn't get dirty"I was told whilst I awaited the arrival of the rest of the family.Once the tables were set up the job began of trying to provide seats for well over a dozen people when you had only six rather flimsy chairs.Ever the "mother of invention" even this failed to beat Nana.Grandad's chair

stayed by the fireside,the table had been pulled into the centre of the room,leaving very little room to circulate around it and then the flaps unfolded to increase its size.The six chairs were equally spaced,three on each side of the table and long wooden planks then laid across them to increase the seating capacity.

At last we could begin to lay the table and my sister,who being seven ears older than me took charge.A freshly laundered white Irish linen tablecloth covered the empty table but it was not long before that had changed and little of the actual cloth remained visible..The cutlery drawer was placed on the table and we started to lay the knives,forks and spoons,before finally putting the serving spoons and large carving and bread knives in the very centre.I can still feel the pain of the cut as my sister tried to pull from my hand the carving knife which I was holding by the blade,as she now proceeded to pull,in doing so the serrated edge,like a saw cut through the palm of my hand.I could feel the warmth as red drops became more of a flow and the lovely clean white cloth took on a crimson hue.I remember my screaming attracting Nanas attention and her words as she came from the kitchen."Oh my goodness,what have you been and done"she said.Unable to make intelligible noises through the tears,I held out my hand,which was quickly wrapped in the tea towel which Nana had in her hand.Once in the kitchen the standard treatment of holding the cut under cold running water was applied,I watched horrified as the pinkish red water ran down the sink whilst the extent of the wound was determined,on examination coupled with the observation"that'll be ok".I,myself,was sure it warranted at least an ambulance with its bell ringing,but it was Christmas and it was the 1950's,you mustn't trouble them they were far

too busy.With this in mind home remedies from the medicine chest had to make do,out came the iodine which was liberally applied, then padded with cotton wool and a bandage made from a strip of old bed linen,the end was torn to enable her to tie it securely.Crisis over,the table cloth replaced,it began all over again,this time with me solely as a spectator,munching away on a consoling chocolate biscuit.much to the disapproval of my sister who claimed favouritism.

****

"As quiet as a church mouse"

****

I had managed to survive till Boxing Day,but only just,my stomach was aching from the amount of rich food appearing and having to be eaten,after all what didn't get used that day would certainly be used as leftovers later.The Christmas afternoon entertainment,likely to be repeated on Boxing Day had been exhausting.Ludo,Snakes and Ladders accompanied by various card games,like Happy Families saw untold laughter,the accusations of "you're cheating" and the inevitable tears,usually because it was me cheating and I still didn't win.Board games exhausted it was on to charades,followed by pass the parcel or a small present would be hidden for the children to find,hide and seek with a bit of a difference.The adults had been full of "the Christmas spirit"since late afternoon,however not the kind that the parish priest would have approved of.Rum,whisky and gin along with barley wine stout,sherry,port and various home made wines had flowed freely,so much so that by "teatime" various people had become soporific and Grandad,having dipped regularly into his supply of milk stout was sat with a rather silly grin,not entirely sure of what was taking place or even what day it was.By about seven o'clock it was decided to get the supper laid out on the table.Having eaten an extensive dinner,roast chicken,all of the trimmings and every seasonal vegetable you could muster,followed by Christmas pudding and mince pies with custard.Not to mention dipping into the bowls of sweets all afternoon whilst playing the games, there were very few crevices left to fill in my stomach or anyone else's.Grandad protesting,"I don't think anyone has room to eat anymore",Nana insisted that they did have,so continued to fill the table once more.As was usual she was correct once the food appeared the temptation was too much.Fairy cakes,mini swiss rolls,mince pies a resplendent decorated Christmas cake,cold meat,piccalilli,pickled onions,pan yan and branston pickle,they all appeared as if by magic as did the likes of Gala pork pie with egg and red salmon,items we only had at Christmas.I tucked hungrily into the cakes and always managed a bowl of jelly and blancmange with Carnation evaporated milk drizzled over it,the adults had sherry trifle and tinned fruit salad,if lucky the evaporated milk would be replaced with single cream.

Suddenly evening was upon us, the day that had been eagerly anticipated,promising so much was over,all that remained was the wrapping paper neatly folded to be used for next year,opened presents and a stomach ache where I had eaten too much.Nana was still working as hard at the beginning as at the end,but why I thought was Christmas Day always shorter than all the other days. Boxing Day,tomorrow, promised to be just as exciting,another chance to celebrate as it was the day of the family party and then the fun really began!

****

"Patience is a virtue,all good things come to he who waits"

****

Nana finally reappeared,worship over for today,I pedalled furiously to meet her as she turned the corner,it was time now to put my new trike,well new to me, away and once back indoors to help with the pressing task of preparing Christmas dinner.A dinner which a normal day would consist of "meat and two veg" now reached gargantuan proportions as pot after pot was filled with water,salted,and then filled with an assortment of vegetables,after all it was Christmas.The fresh vegetables, of which there were far too many, I had helped prepare earlier,peeling potatoes,parsnips,turnips and swede,scraping carrots,removing the outer leaves of brussel sprouts.Nearby in the gas fuelled copper of boiling water the Christmas pudding bubbled away happily in the hot and steamy kitchen.The chicken which we had said our farewells to a few days prior had been prepared the day before Christmas Eve,stuffed with homemade stuffing made from,bread crumbs,parsley,and onion and was now resident in the oven and

137

starting to roast,soon to be accompanied by the roasting potatoes,Anyone not lucky enough to have fattened their own chickens often had a piece of beef or a capon for the main meal,purchased from the local butcher,Mr,Jones,Potatoes by now lay cheek by jowl with the browning bird and basted regularly with fat from the chicken,which had been basted itself in lard or dripping,had began to brown and crisp up nicely.My task was to lay the table ready to accept the surfeit of rich food,plates,knives forks and spoons,the salt,pepper and mustard pots,white crisp napkins only brought out on special occasions all adorned a white linen tablecloth.By twelve thirty,a little later than normal,dinner arrived on the table,Grandad carved the chicken which had arrived on a large platter surrounded by piles of roast potatoes and stuffing,he gave a leg each to himself and Dad,placing white breast meat on the remaining plates at the table before adding a portion of stuffing and roast spuds to each plate.Nana added some of each vegetable to each plate,which you were expected to eat and not waste",waste not,want not"being the motto.Thick gravy made with gravy browning and the meat juices from the chicken was then liberally poured over the food on the plates.Grace,as was normal, was recited,but before eating we all pulled the Tom Smith's crackers that had been laid at each place at the table.Simple cardboard tubes with an even simpler"snap" covered in crepe paper of various hues,each one with a motif stuck on the outside,inside a moto,a joke and a cheap trinket,maybe marbles,pencil sharpener,keyring or an infuriating puzzle and that most important of all,a brightly coloured paper hat."Come on eat up before it gets cold,we were urged,Christmas was the only time you could talk at the table and as I pulled my crepe paper covered cracker with its foil holly motif laughter and shrieks of joy were in abundance.Paper hats appeared on every head,many not removed till bedtime,the small insignificant trinkets had fallen from the crackers,many on to the floor, and the schoolboy mottos and jokes added to the frivolity.dinner,at Christmas,was the happiest meal of the year,no sooner had we finished than the washing up was done,my job was to wipe up the items as they were cleaned.nobody had the stomach for pudding without taking a breather and the time taken to wash up was just the break needed.whilst Nana boiled milk in an enamel saucepan before adding Bird's custard powder from a red,blue and yellow tin,then sugar, to make the creamy custard to accompany the rich Christmas pudding.I carried the small bowls to the waiting table,followed by an enormous jug of steaming custard,the last person in was Nana.The fruit pudding had been turned out from its bowl onto an enamel plate and steeped in a miniature bottle of brandy,a sprig of holly inserted in the top and the alcohol ignited.The bluish flame flickered and danced over the surface of the pudding as it was carried in,before extinguishing itself,the pudding then being ready to serve.Excitement mounted as I peered intently as each knife cut was made,waiting to see the signs of greaseproof paper,I would say "next piece please" if no paper was apparent certain that I would shortly be the owner of a much coveted silver sixpence if i waited long enough.Pudding finished,sixpences uncovered,we had a final mince pie accompanied by a wee glass of sherry for the adults,for myself it was homemade lemonade or ginger beer,as we huddled around the little bakelite radio to listen to the Queen's speech as three o'clock arrived..

When the speech was over,the adults spent a while discussing the implications of what had been said,over a much needed cup of tea before the board games were brought out and at long last I was able to indulge in a chocolate or toffee from one of the glass bowls on the sideboard.The little bowls gradually emptied,the box of Turban dates was attacked by the little white fork which was in it to stop your fingers becoming sticky,the sugar coated figs I did not fancy and the sugar almonds I was told to suck and not bite"they will ruin your teeth Nana would say",why then did they buy them I asked cheekily

****

"Waste not,want not,there are people starving out there"

****

I awoke with a start,no idea of the hour,I seemed to have been in bed or hours,I certainly felt wide awake as though I had been asleep for along time but it was still dark apart from the glint of the moon shining through a crack in the old blackout curtains.It was then that I thought I heard the sound of bells.Instinctively but in a slight panic I retreated as deep down under the bedclothes and heavy eiderdown as possible,aware that if I saw Father Christmas,or he saw me, my presents would probably not arrive and the great day would be rather bleak.I listened, then realised the bells were in fact from St Faith's Church, summoning the parishioners to attend midnight mass and I had been woken by Nana closing the front door as she left home to take part in the traditional service leaving Grandad as my custodian.By the time she returned I must have fallen back to sleep,as I didn't hear her come in,intermittently rousing,waiting for any sound or movement to suggest the great man had been,the signal to go downstairs.I waited and waited,everybody was in bed,every so often I nodded off but there was still no sound,had I missed him,more worrying had he missed me.The temptation to creep silently down stairs became too much and eventually it got the better of me.Outside in Leesland Road I could here the chink of glass bottles heralding the arrival of the Co-op milkman,yes,even on Christmas Day,there was no rest for the wicked Nana would say,but it escaped me as to why the milkman and the postman,who delivered later,were any more wicked than any other

140

workers who had the day off.More to the point however was that if the milkman was delivering Santa must have been.Thus it was that Nana found me sometime later,sat in front of an unlit fire,in a cold semi dark room,waiting in my dressing gown and slippers to open my presents but their didn't seem to be any,had I been missed.The stockings hanging from the mantlepiece seemed to be full enough but there was no big present.My stocking was taken down from its hook and handed to me to empty whilst Nana busied herself with lighting a fire to warm the room,the fact that it was icy cold and a white frost covered the ground outside had escaped my notice.The warmth of anticipated joy had more than compensated for that,but I still didn't seem to have that big present,more importantly there were no clues or evidence as to where it might be or even if there was a big present.I feverishly unpacked my bulging stocking,it was amazing just how much went in to such a humble piece of hosiery,an orange,an apple,an assortment of brazils,walnuts and almonds,a ten shilling note.A pair of socks,a pack of white initialed handkerchiefs,colouring book,pencils and a small Rowneys water colour tin with a red handled paint brush.I remember I was so excited,but still no big present,I knew there wasn't one for me as I had checked all the labels whilst feeling them to work out their contents,there wasn't one with my name on it.."Morning lad,Happy Christmas" said Grandad as he came down the stairs.no doubt detecting the disappointment in my voice as I replied "Happy Christmas Grandad". Nana had by now made a pot of tea and was setting about the day's breakfast preparations before dressing in her"Sunday best",once again to go to the early morning church service at eight o'clock.."Come on Charlie,can't you see the boy's waiting"she said,"I've got to go,be quick else I will be late".Grandad took a slurp of his hot tea before getting up from his chair,made his way outside and I patiently watched from the window as instructed.I was not dressed and it was too cold to go outside,although Grandad's attire was no better defence from the bitter chill than mine.He opened the shed door,slowly entered and with a yellow toothy grin on his rugged face,under his ever present flat cap, re-emerged pushing a tricycle.It was what I had been dreaming of,although refurbished and repainted that maroon and cream conveyance with its large box,with a chrome handle on it was the best present I had ever had.Breakfast was a bowl of porridge"to keep out the cold"mixed with a spoonful of sweet Fussels condensed milk,I didn't have time for toast I needed to get on my trike and I still wasn't dressed.Washing and dressing took forever,not helped by me putting on my best clothes,well it was Christmas, only to be told,"if your going outside put your normal clothes on and wrap up warm you'll need to keep your best ones for later".As Nana left for church I was indeed "wrapped up warm",I was almost too restricted to pedal and as I accompanied her as far as the corner of Norman Road,as soon as she disappeared down Tribe Road off came the balaclava and scarf which I placed in the box on the back of the trike.I spent the time waiting for her return riding up and down the pavement,excitedly shouting to any random passerby,of which there were few apart from a lone postman"Happy Christmas,look what I've got".

****

God gives and God takes it away"

****

It was Christmas Eve,tomorrow would be Christmas Day,excitement was filling the air with the anticipation of giving and receiving presents,My Nana always said ''it is better to give than receive"for some reason I was unable to agree,me receiving presents was the sole reason for Christmas,apart of course for the birth of our saviour.

but with only a small amount saved through the year the presents given by me were by necessity small.many presents were laboriously homemade,by ingenuity we always found a way to make something special and we could all do it with no,or very little cost to the giver.I would decorate small tins or wooden boxes by glueing cut out pictures from old magazines,once dry Grandad would give it a coat of clear varnish.Another favourite would be to make and paint a little plaster of paris figure in the form of an animal which had been turned out of a rubber mould.On one occasion I had used an old empty sherry bottle,which I covered in plaster of paris then painstaking pressed small shells,cockle,topshells,turret shells and small pieces of coloured glass that I had collected from the beach,into it before it dried.I popped a candle into the top and the crude lamp was complete,the value was the fact that the effort put into producing it was far more than any possible monetary value.Similarly a bowl made up of papier mache,little bits of newspaper soaked in glue,made from flour and water,the layers built up,then once dry brightly painted.
****

"There's none so blind as those who cannot see"

****

Drinking my cup of steaming sweet cocoa,thank goodness sugar was no longer rationned,it was almost bedtime,the soporific effect of the warming drink risked it being spilt on my clean pyjamas as my eyes began to slowly close.This,however, was part of the plan to get me into bed early,before the rotund figure,with his white beard and red cloak,drove his reindeer hauled sleigh across the twinkling stars of the wintry sky on his annual visit.The whole of Christmas Eve had been perpetual motion,there was no time to stop,there was just too much to do culminating in the family decorating the Christmas tree,which always took place at tea time the day before the celebrations began in earnest.Fetching and carrying were my chores as Nana asked me to run down the corner shop for last minute requirements,it was always the most obvious item that had been forgotten.Mr and Mrs.Horne's corner grocers shop was packed to burst,everything you had forgotten to buy when you had done your weekly grocery shop they had,if it wasn't in stock they would get it in stock especially for you,nothing was too much trouble and always done with a smile.From their shop I would return home only to be sent across the road to Mrs Sands little florist shop,as with many of these little shops it was the front room of her house which had been adapted.I would be sent to obtain a twig of mistletoe to be hung over the front door of number 80,and to see if the holly wreaths were ready for collection.There were normally four wreaths,three for the graves in the cemetery and one for the front door of the house,meanwhile,Mr Shepherd with his faithful old horse and cart would be delivering his final fruit,vegetables and nuts to his grateful customers,most giving him a packet of cigarettes,or other small gifts to thank him for the service he had provided to them for the past year.All tradesmen that delivered regularly to the doorstep of the house come rain or shine would be treated in the same way,a little reward for their reliable service.Back home Nana would be in the kitchen,or scullery,making final touches to the chickens that had been plucked and "drawn" the day before.The stuffing,made with fresh parsley from the garden,onions from the allotments and breadcrumbs made from drying stale bread in the oven which was then crushed with the rolling pin was then "stuffed" under the breast of the chicken.Each stuffed chicken was then given a dusting of flour and covered in greaseproof paper,the washed giblets wrapped separately as they would be needed for stock,once ready each allocated to one of the annual recipients.As the evening arrived the chickens would be duly collected,Uncle Dennis would arrive for his,Dad would take ours when he arrived to pick me up,and the last one Nana would take up the road to Uncle Bert and Auntie Ada,when she joined them to watch Coronation Street.We didn't have a television set of our own so every evening Nana would walk up to number 100 to watch the news at seven o'clock followed by Ena Sharples and her cronies over a biscuit and cup of tea..Along with the chicken each recipient would get a christmas pudding,in a white ceramic bowl,covered and tied with a white pudding cloth.Whilst this was happening the kitchen was still a hive of activity,final preparations were well underway, next thing on the list of jobs was to make the various flavoured Rowntrees jellies,usually strawberry and orange,a blackcurrant one turned into a milk jelly by adding Ideal evaporated milk,in various moulds shaped as rabbits,castles,or crowns Brown and Polsons blancmange was setting in chocolate,strawberry or vanilla flavours.During the process of dissolving the jelly in hot water,having removed it from its small green box,it was exceedingly difficult when tearing up the squares not to divert a square or two into my hungry stomach,resulting in a great deal of scolding,and not one or two stomach aches.As the activity reached fever pitch,me getting more in the way than usual,seeing what delicacies I could have a sneaky taste of,after a light dinner Dad had whisked me off with my sister to do last minute shopping in Portsmouth.Driving down to Gosport we parked the car in Mumby Road before walking along past the bus ranks to board the Gosport Ferry,alighting for the short journey across the harbour to Portsmouth.My little legs could barely keep up as we walked"up the Hard", alongside the tall dockyard wall before arriving in Charlotte Street with its atmospheric market.The wheeled barrows,and piles of crates and boxes groaned under the weight of the festive fare,each one surrounded by costermongers and barrow boys imploring the gathered throng to purchase their wares,"two packets a pound,"could be heard as they sold packets of figs,Turban dates or boxes of Politi turkish delight.".Similarly you were encouraged to purchase fruit,"get yer bananas here,lovely red apples,sweet juicy pears and ripe pineapples for half a crown"Invariably persuasion worked wonders and heavy laden shoppers carried home far more than they really needed but rationing during the wartime meant this new glut of cheaper produce drove over indulgence.

Amongst the barrows,tasty seasonal treats would be hawked the hot hestnut stall,the brazier an added attraction on a cold day,a man selling brown sticky toffee apples or large wands of pink sugary candy floss.A colourfully dressed individual churning out tinny Christmas music from a barrel organ was accompanied by a tiny dressed monkey perched on top of it.Almost asleep,aching feet,tired legs we returned laden like pack horses,at last the Christmas victuals were complete.Whilst we had been away,the real reason for getting us out of the house was apparent,Nana had wrapped the Christmas parcels.We arrived home just as the first of the family arrived to collect their Christmas dinners,once they had gone,before Nana went up to Uncle Bert and Auntie Ada we had one thing left to do,that involved more exciting final preparations.

***.

"The final straw that broke the camel's back"

****

During the course of the day,in between all the events taking place someone had managed to unearth from the back of the understairs cupboard the Christmas tree decorations,not without a certain amount of dust.Having had a cup of tea,accompanied by hot toasted,buttered crumpets,once home,I was despatched,accompanied by Grandad,to collect the tree from Shepherd's shop opposite Nanas.Placed in a zinc pail of damp earth,covered in red crepe paper,the six foot tree,was positioned on the floor in front of the front room window.Decorating could now commence glass hand painted baubles,clear plastic stars and icicles,all tied to the tree with cotton,silver tin candle clips with red and white candles.I would carefully pass these items,then shook the silver,gold,red,blue and green tinsel and silver lame to remove the layer of dust,followed by cotton wool which when teased out thinly represented snow.Electric lights we did not have,as we still used gas for lighting so inevitably the candles would have provided illumination although rarely lit due to the risk of accidents!

As the tree was being finished with a topping out ceremony using an old,battered fairy which looked as though it was as old as Christmas itself,Nana and Grandad reminisced of past Christmases they and the little doll had seen.All day there had been a constant procession of family,neighbours and tradesmen dropping by,each offered a glass of Harveys Bristol Cream sherry,VP fino or amontillado sherry and a hot mince pie,all offering us seasons greetings.I was treated to a glass of Corona orangeade and a peppermint cream,the latter being made by adding peppermint essence to the leftover royal icing that had been used to ice the Christmas cake,just to keep me quiet.As everyone drifted away,the tree decorated,preparations completed,Coronation Street viewed,the clock was approaching eight o'clock or thereabouts and I was fighting sleep,desperate to not have to go to bed but eventually giving in just in case Santa came early.Thus it was that you now found me sleepily reminding Nana and Grandad to ensure the mince pie and wee dram was left in the fireplace,to make sure the fire was out and finally I pinned my stocking above the open fire,it never crossed my mind that with all the wee drams consumed it was surprising Santa arrived anywhere on time,or even at all! Finally I climbed up the dark narrow stairs,I knelt on the cold floorboards, offered up my prayers for the family,then almost as an afterthought included everyone else,finishing off with the Lord's Prayer.I climbed into the luke warm bed,the hot water bottle having beat me to it and soon fell asleep,but for how long I wasn't sure.

****

"Actions speak louder than words"

****

There were two days left,there was still so much to do and now there seemed very little time left in which to do it,every year was the same,but we always managed to have Christmas on December the twenty fifth.Archie Shepherd could be seen slowly wending his way up Leesland Road,the faithful old horse pulling the cart,piled high with vegetables and fruit knowing exactly when and where to stop and when to move on.It was Christmas and like all of us he had his treats,carrots,apples and an odd polo mint or two..At this time of year Archie was in great demand for a skill that to some was unsavoury,but nevertheless somebody needed to perform.He took no satisfaction from it, when outside some houses Archie,in dirty flat cap,trousers tucked into wellington boots,long grey coat and leather apron he would knock and go in.Moments later he would come and return to the cart and continue to dispense the vegetables weighing them on a large set of brass scales."Three bob please,that's four you've given me"he would say as he tipped up the leather cash bag to find the change which he handed over saying"that's a shilling change".This was the one day of the Christmas holidays when I felt uncomfortable and a little sad.Every day since April when the little yellow fluffy chicks had arrived

148

from Dittman and Malpass in the high street I had fed them,thrown slugs and snails in their run as a treat,thrown in handfuls of corn and spent many hours talking to them as they clucked and pecked their way around.I had eaten their eggs for breakfast and now after Mr Shepherd's visit I was expected to eat them for dinner,strangely however it just seemed the normal thing to do.They suddenly went from lively fowl to lifeless creatures hanging by their feet from a nail in the backyard wall,blood dripping from their beaks,expressionless eyes awaiting the next stage in their lives short journey.Inside the house,a little white behind the gills,I stood in silence,slightly numb I tried to not look in the yard but to assist Nana in other happier preparations.There was still plenty to do ,the clock was still ticking so attention turned to icing the Christmas cake.I was sent to fetch the tin of cake decorations,stored from previous years from the sideboard,the cake was put on a large white plate and we began.Firstly for the final time holes were made in the top of the rich dark fruit cake and a few drops of brandy dripped in,whilst this was taking place I fetched a jar of apricot jam from the cupboard by the fireplace.Left to stand to soak up the alcohol it was thirty minutes later before I could start my first task,to spread the entire cake surface of the cake with the apricot jam whilst Nana began to make the almond paste,or marzipan,from ground almonds,icing sugar and egg yolk all mixed into a ball to be rolled out with a rolling pin to make a kind of tablecloth.My mouth watered at the prospect of consuming any trimmings once it had been placed like a cover on the sticky layer of jam I had previously applied to the cake..Any left over was fashioned into marzipan fruits decorated with angelica,crystallised lemon and orange and touched with red from the cochineal bottle.The royal icing was then prepared and liberally spread around the cake,a fork used to make little peaks giving the impression of snow and little silver balls added to make the words "Happy Christmas".Completing the decoration,chalk figures,recycled year in and year out,were taken from the tin and added to the top,a snowbaby on a toboggan,a snowman,Father Christmas on his sleigh and a vivid green Christmas tree made from what looked like the top of a bottle brush,all had seen better days but had become part of the tradition.The final touch was a recycled red and white fringed paper cake frill in gold and red,secured in place with a daub of the remaining icing.Any icing left in the bowl had an addition of peppermint essence mixed in and then formed into flat round peppermint creams,at which point I was allowed to lick the bowl of any residue left.Dinner time intervened,the cake was put away in the larder,we ate and then I would

sit and uncomfortably watch as the tin bath was brought into the scullery.Nana and Grandad would bring in the lifeless chickens,one by one,then commence plucking the feathers by hand,an unpleasant task,which left the fingers extremely sore the aim was to remove all the feathers without tearing the skin.I recall the acrid smell as the feathers,of little use,ended up being burnt on the living room fire,at least it was only once a year.whilst Nana eviscerated the poor now naked fowl.Heads were deftly removed,careful to leave as much neck as possible,the innards drawn,careful not to puncture the gallbladder,the bitter contents would render the rest of the giblets which had been retained unusable,then finally the feet were removed and scrubbed.Almost all the chicken was used,after all why be wasteful when money was scarce and it was edible.The dressed bird was then washed,dried,dusted with flour and the ready to cook bird trussed for the oven,the legs and wings tied with twine then secured with metal meat skewers.Tomorrow would see the finishing touches applied,the next twenty four hours were designed to tire me out so that I would sleep well and not be awake when Father Christmas arrived on Christmas Night.

"When in Rome do as the Romans"

Dogs were always in our home and Oxford Road was the first home when one crossed the doorstep,he,a long haired golden retriever arrived on the scene before the year I was born.In fact he was bought for my sister so that she would have some kind of company but I remember that he would do anything for my Dad and he was obedient to a fault.He was named somewhat dubiously with a name that is no longer accepted,how he got the name none us really knew.He was an attentive animal and would accompany us on most occasions before Mum died,we would go to Stokes Bay where would swim out to chase the stones as we skimmed them over the water,he would also give me a ride on his back around the garden.He waited obediently in Privet Park one day, when Dad forgot he had taken him with him and left him behind,there he was sat obediently where he was told to stay when Dad returned some time later.He shed hair everywhere,long honey golden strands that stuck to your clothes,he smelt"doggy" at times but he always smiled.he strutted along on his walks with his tail held high,that was until just before Christmas in 1955,when being a rascal he blotted his copybook..He nearly always accompanied us in the car but on this occasion as we were going shopping in Charlotte Street fruit and vegetable market,across the harbour in Portsmouth,it was felt that it would be sensible to leave him at home.Unable to take him with us he was left with a handful of Spillers Shapes dog biscuits and his water bowl,hi old eiderdown for him to sleep on,in fact all that was necessary for a dog to be content,however we had overlooked one small detail in our hurry to get out,so that we wouldn't be away too long for him to be on his own.We need now to go back to the evening of two days before.As the holiday approached our food was all ordered and arrangements made for its collection..We were looking forward to the festive dinner with the chicken supplied from Nana's on Christmas eve but this year was a little different it was to be a first not planned but the result of a stroke of good luck.Turkeys were just appearing in the local butchers shops,they were a new type of poultry,very expensive and only bought by the better off,it would be several years before the working man had one at his table.What a surprise,therefore when Dad arrived home with a giant turkey,plucked and drawn,feet still attached,announcing he had won it in John Hunts Christmas Raffle.The excitement of such a win was unbridled as Dad hung the lifeless bird on the back of the conservatory door,the coolest place in the house as we had no refrigerator and being winter and the conservatory glass it was extremely cold..We should have realised from the glint in the dog's eye,the fixation on the conservatory door and the drool hanging from his lips that the turkey was a great sense of interest to our beloved best friend.It certainly was not a sensible action on our part then, to lock the dog in the conservatory along with the turkey,as you can imagine in his mind it was as if all his birthdays were come in one,an opportunity not to be lightly dismissed.He needed no second invitation it looked delicious,far tastier than dog biscuits and he could consume it at leisure with nobody at home.On our return all was quiet,the dog unusually didn't come to greet us when we opened the conservatory door.as we peered in to see him our horrified faces only too clearly reflected the scene of blood and carnage that greeted us.An exceedingly happy dog greeted us,wagging his tail,laughing,through bloody lips,strangely enough he wasn't hungry that evening,he did avoid us but it was difficult to blame him entirely for our stupid oversight. Oh well it would have to be chicken again,turkey would still be a treat for several years later,but the dog enjoyed it,even if he was unable to tell us what it tasted like.

****

''Get it out of your system''

****

Monday morning arrived,I was up early as normal,it was still bitterly cold and apart from the continuing festive preparations the normal weekly chores still had to be completed,everyday life had to go on even if it was Christmas at the end of the week.This Monday was no different from any other,after all cleanliness was next to godliness and this was a very godly time of year.The preparations we had already made seemed rather inadequate,the five days we had begun with had now shrunk to just three,the amount of work to be done seemed no less than when we had originally started and the bathtub used for the task of washing was needed for Tuesday for something entirely different.Whilst Nana performed her normal household chores,the washing,hanging it on the line to dry,preparing dinner and general cleaning I was tasked with little jobs to supposedly aid the smooth run up to the festivities.I checked the little counters in the red box which contained the Ludo and Snakes and Ladders boards,red,blue,yellowand green,I checked the playing cards for Happy Families and Snap to ensure none were missing.The holly sprigs with their glossy pointed green leaves crowned with tight clusters of red berries gleaned from the local cemetery were mine to embellish with a light dusting of silver and gold glitter,ready to place onto the mantelpiece above the open fire,keeping one piece back for the Christmas pudding.The little pressed vaseline glass bowls were retrieved from the sideboard,wiped clean,then ready to be filled with,Bluebird assorted toffees,Maynards wine gums,Roses chocolates and pink and white sugar Jordan almonds,placed back on the sideboard for me to offer to visitors when the time came, but not to be eaten by me.Opening the cupboard doors I looked longingly at the packets of assorted biscuits and sweets which screamed at me to be eaten,not however was this likely to be before Christmas Day.My next job was to check the tree decorations,real glass baubles,tinsel strands,cotton wool,candles with holders,and the all important fairy for the top of tree,but that would have to be put off till Christmas Eve as unfortunately after dinner I developed a much unwanted migraine.It seemed a pretty boring day,doing chores but it only enhanced the anticipation which was part of the build up to Christmas.As the day wore on the postman added to the cards we had already received.Mr Chase the rent man collected his money and wishing us a "Merry Christmas" accepted a small glass of Bristol cream sherry.Various other tradespeople,baker,grocer,coalman and logman would make their final deliveries and be offered a small glass of sherry and passed a small brown envelope with their Christmas Box,usually a brown ten shilling note.Traditionally "tipping" had been on Boxing Day but now it was the last delivery before Christmas,or Christmas Day for the postman and milkman,everyone was rewarded for the excellent service they had given all year,any misdemeanours wiped out and forgotten,after all it was Christmas,it was the season of goodwill.The postman,milkman,bread man,Co-op grocery man,Mr Stanley the log man,the coalman,dustman and Mr Shepherd the fruit and vegetable man,the last named to play a prominent part in the following days activities,all received that small token of appreciation for their years efforts.As the day drew towards evening,the washing done,hung on the line,now back indoors but still damp so now hanging from the wooden clothes horse stood in front of the coal fire.Nana started to make time to do some baking,a rare thing on a Monday,but the supply of mince pies had to be replenished after the inroads made on them by the carol singers and sausage rolls were needed for Christmas Eve.Gazing out the front door the dark evening greeted a red glow slowly coming down the road,pausing frequently,every now and then the chink of a bell as the hot chestnut man,his brazier balanced on a hand cart,dispensed a few hot chestnuts into a little white paper bag for a few pence.In the glow from the gas lamps a few snowflakes fell like dust,only to have gone by morning to be replaced by the endless frost and icy ground.

As the smells of cooking rose up the stairs,even with a headache my mouth watered,excitement and anticipation mounting,only to be slightly dampened   by the events of the following day.probably the least welcome day of the festive period,but it was still part of our traditional Christmas.

****

"You've bitten off more than you can chew"

****

She would always have a kind word delivered in a deep, throaty,gravelly tone,accompanied by a persistent cough I remember her well, dressed in a housecoat, holding up the flowers at arms length and looking at the arrangement approvingly,then looking at you to see if you,also, approved of her.handiwork.She always had a cigarette either between the two fingers on her left hand or dangling from the corner of her mouth,her greying hair was stained yellow from the nicotine of the endless smoke.Mr and Mrs Sands owned the little flower shop,she always there to serve,he,a bespectacled man with hair either side of the bald patch on his head could be seen wearing a long grey mackintosh, riding a rusty old trades bike to who knows where She also wore glasses,hers with tortoise shell frames and I remember she had what was known as a caste in her eye and known to like a drop of gin,as her breath would testify.The most memorable thing about her however was that gravelly voice derived from her constant smoking and the hollow cough that accompanied it.

****

"You expect me to do it at the drop of a hat"

****

The days had passed quickly,much to my surprise,but there was still no snow which we always looked forward to,fern like ice patterns had appeared on the inside of my bedroom window it was so cold,there was no central heating meaning it was as cold inside as outside at night time and quite often well into the day..Although there was no snow outside,the hoar frosts were often so heavy that it looked like a covering of snow I could see my breath as I exhaled,it was like a white mist even inside the house.I hurriedly skipped downstairs to the little dining room which was already warming up where Nana had thoughtfully lit the small fire to take the chill off of the room. I was soon crouched over the now roaring fire,warming my hands on a mug of tea whilst waiting for a bowl of piping hot porridge to arrive on the table.From the scullery,however,it was not the smell of porridge cooking that was wafting out this morning,but a smell of more savoury proportions,as the large ox tongue which had been soaked in brine overnight,was now in a large pot accompanied by an assorted mix of carrots,onions,peppercorns,bay leaf and cloves,with which it would

156

simmer for the next four hours.By the time I had drunk my mug of tea the porridge had duly arrived,steam curling from its surface a spoon or two of golden syrup from the green and gold Tate and Lyle tin was added Treacle or Fussells condensed milk was often a holiday treat,making the normal sweet porridge so much sweeter it was verging on sickly,but as with most children I loved it.The only shops open,would be the florists,as it was Sunday,the Lord's day,you were expected to go to a place of worship,in our case Saint Faith's church it was the day of rest and manual working was frowned upon,as was shopping.It did result in forward planning for the Sunday being extremely important,particularly as regards to meals.In fact in those times planning was a vital necessity throughout the whole week,there was much to be done and very few "labour saving gadgets"to help to do it.A knock came on the door,on opening it Mrs Sands,cigarette in mouth,stood holding the four holly wreaths that had been ordered,one which we needed for the front door was placed around the large brass knocker,the other three for our outing to the cemetery later that afternoon.Along with the wreaths she had also brought a small sprig of mistletoe,pale lime green leaves and white waxy berries,which was an important "risque" ingredient for the grown ups celebrations.An opportunity to kiss someone they would not have done at other times of the year,was unlikely to be missed,but during this festive season it provided just the needed excuse to take advantage of the pagan tradition,which spilled over into the christian festival.On the Sunday before Christmas the traditional roast was usually dispensed with and a simpler dinner,of a steak and kidney pie or beef sausages would suffice,after all you had to leave room for the rich food which would be the signature for the rest of the holidays.As momentum gathered there was one activity which was never pushed aside,that was the church service,the carol services were looked forward to with relish,deafening renditions of popular carols resounded from every church and could even be heard from the carol singers which frequented our doorsteps during the dark evenings.The nativity scene,with the crib,baby and farm animals was the real reason for the celebrations suitably revered by the congregation as they filed into the church,which always seemed to grow in numbers at this time of year.By the time dinner was served the ox tongue was well cooked.It was removed from the saucepan and placed on a metal plate to cool sufficiently so it could be skinned,I can remember vividly the sandpaper like texture of the skin which was removed in strips before the final preparations.Once skinned the now naked tongue was placed back on the plate,the wooden breadboard was then placed on top of it,then several handy house bricks were used to press the cooked tongue.All prepared,we left it to press for several hours.By now we had dressed in our "Sunday Best" and reverently clutching three of the holly wreaths,careful not to dislodge the red berries,we walked up Leesland Road to the cemetery to place them on the waiting graves.In the older part of the cemetery,no longer used for burials,the smallest wreath found a home on Uncle Phil's grave,only a babe when tuberculosis ended his life in the early 20th century.Picking our way through the often ancient graves,Nana snipped a few sprigs from the holly trees to add to our own decorations at home,to which I added some large fir cones I found underneath the trees,and some ivy with its black berries from this older part of the cemetery.I constantly kept pestering Nana to carry it all and then when I did complained that the holly kept pricking me.Having crossed into the newer part of the cemetery,on the opposite side of Anns Hill Road I laid the larger wreath on my mum's grave,standing head bowed for a moment or two before skipping off only to be told in a stern voice"to have some respect there are people here",still not understanding clearly what death really meant.Nana in the meantime laid the last wreath on the grave next to mums in which Grandad was interred.Darkness was falling as we left,there was a chill in the wind as we hurried back home for the rest of the afternoon,to be spent with me "assisting" in putting up the paper decorations that I had made the previous day.They were nothing elaborate, simple items,bands of crepe paper twisted into chains as they were pinned from corner to corner of the room,others were made from coloured paper strips glued at each end to form the links of multi coloured chains.These were added to the Chinese paper concertina lanterns,turquoise and pink,beautifully decorated with flowers and peacocks and hung every year from the ceiling.The ivy,holly and fir cones I had collected that afternoon were placed around the pictures,sideboard and mantelpiece to make them look more festive.The finishing touches were put to the mince pies baked earlier with a dusting of fine icing sugar,little sausage rolls were put in the oven to bake and last of all from the store cupboard appeared a large Lyons chocolate swiss roll which was placed on a rectangular silver cake board recycled from previous years.Hard to believe the cake boards,which were silver foiled cardboard, were washed and dried when Christmas was over and stored till the following year.Turning our attention to the opened swiss roll it was placed on the board and liberally covered in chocolate butter icing,coloured and flavoured with Cadbury's Bournville cocoa powder,before being spiked with a fork to look like wood bark,then sprinkled with icing sugar to represent snow..Once decorated with sprigs of holly and a chalk reindeer or two it provided us with a very acceptable yule log.A mug of Horlicks,Cocoa or Ovaltine accompanied by a couple of Cadbury's chocolate fingers was the ideal end to the day as we sat by the fire,listening to Christmas carols on the little bakelite radio before bed.Gradually I became sleepier as I watched Nana wrapping and tying with wool layer after layer of old wrapping paper,saved from previous years, around an item I would not know the Identity of till the day after tomorrow.This was to be the pass the parcel prize for Boxing Day when the whole extended family arrived to join in.Now however it was time for bed and I would not have to wait much longer to see what Santa Claus had brought me.

****

''I'll give a taste of your own medicine young man''

****

I awoke early,very rarely did we lie in,although it was very tempting to snuggle deep in the bed clothes on the cold winter mornings,like everyone else Christmas meant extra work for all and that included me. It was the first day of the Christmas holidays,it seemed a lifetime before the big day,although it was only five more busy days.I longed for the cold frosty mornings to turn into cold snowy ones but this only happened on January and February mornings,very rarely in December.A white Christmas with snowmen and snowballs was a
dream but the nearest I can remember was a few wayward snowflakes drifting across the sky on one Christmas Eve.With this prospect out and my friends experiencing the same in their homes,with their own families,it resulted in once breakfast was over I would be found walking with Nana to the shops in Whitworth Road.As we made our way down Leesland Road delicious smells wafted from open doors,squeals of anticipated delight rang in the air and season greetings were liberally imparted to all that I met.There was always an air of excitement at this time of year and no matter how much or how little we had we were happy and joyful.Everywhere the signs were slowly appearing,the odd coloured light,the glimpse of a paper chain through a parlour window or a card on a window cill. The uniformed postmen carrying heavy canvas sacks,hurried,bent in half,between the never ending

doors,auxiliary postmen,mostly non uniformed but badged students made up for any shortfall of staff,cards appeared on the doormat two or three times a day as Christmas grew closer.Impatience was beginning to show.,did we have to buy more stamps and did I have to lick them and stick them to the envelopes.These were the last cards to be posted but they should arrive at their destinations in time,after all we had a Christmas Day post delivery in 1956.Leaving the post office"Merry Christmas"ringing in our ears I walked across to Dyer's Dairy shop where we placed our cream and egg order for collection on Christmas Eve,a job on the day for me to do if I kept to the pavement,stopped at the kerb and looked both ways before crossing the roads en route. The milk,we had gold top for custard as a treat and the glass bottles of orange juice with green foil tops would be delivered by the Co-op milkman,who also worked on Christmas Day.Next door to the little dairy,with its marble topped counters was a little newsagents,where we would pay our paper bill,nearly everyone had their newspapers delivered,the payment was acknowledged with a small paper receipt torn from a heavy ledger,listing customers names,addresses,the titles of the papers they had and how much they owed.The shops were all decorated with red green and gold foil "Merry Christmas" banners hanging in their windows,the windows covered in a white wash around the edges to make them seasonal,an odd strand of tinsel laid nonchalantly in their window display and a small glass bauble decorated tree stood unlit in a corner.The last call was a detour to see Uncle Will,a jolly "pickwickian" type of man and Auntie Flo,his wife, who was not in the best of health and lived in Vernon Road.The visit completed,me better of by a shilling,we made our way to Mr Jones the butcher,whose shop was on the corner of Vernon Road and Whitworth Road.Here,Christmas certainly seemed to be happening.The chrome rails above the shop window and behind the counter were laden with fresh meat, half pigs,hind and fore quarters of beef,rabbits,chicken,capon and goose,all being prepared for collection for the Christmas table.The hustle and bustle of the butchers cutting joints was frantic,rolling beef and wielding heavy wooden fat bashers to flatten the cod fat ready to go around the beef joints,plenty of fat helped the basting when it was in the oven as well as adding to the flavour.Marble slabs were piled high with large grey ox-tongues,bunches of fresh parsley added splashes of green,between trays of pork and beef sausages and sausage meat.We had come to place our final order which would be collected on Christmas Eve or delivered by the butcher's boy on his delivery bike. Nana had saved all year with the meat club,a couple of shilling a week or what you could comfortably afford,thus there was nothing to pay unless you had overspent.The shilling was"burning a hole in my pocket"I was itching to spend it but was advised that I should keep it, to add it to any other money received over Christmas,then buy something I really wanted and not to waste it,not that I considered sweets being a waste.It did however instill us the idea that if you saved hard you could buy almost anything you desired,patience was indeed a virtue.

****

"You've hit the nail on the head"

****

It was only dinner time,a lot had been achieved but there was half a day to go,what was Nana to do with an impatient little boy like me,well,as always,she had a simple answer.Dinner eaten and with everything cleared away she would produce several items which I snatched at eagerly,at the same time Grandad decided to retire to the parlour "for some peace and quiet",more correctly termed"as having a nap".There were packets of balloons,which took all the puff we could muster to inflate,in fact more than I could muster having to rely on Grandad when he reappeared.A packet of coloured sticky paper strips turned into paper chains,white cartridge paper became dancing snowmen,sheets of coloured crepe paper turned into various festive shapes,tubes of coloured glitter and glue added a little bit of glamour.It was time to start making the homemade Christmas decorations to augment those we had stored from previous years,as few were bought ready made.maybe one or two if there was some money left over once everything had been bought The first items were Christmas cards for the family,hand drawn or traced ,coloured and decorated with the various red,blue,silver,gold and glitter,that was glued on.Spare crepe paper was cut into strips,ready to twist into paper chains,these supplemented by the glued paper strips that had been intertwined into links.Other crepe paper was folded and using round ended scissors cut into dancing men or angels to go with the snowmen in the window, being careful not to get them wet as the ink used to colour the paper was not"fast"and would run..Chinese lanterns were then made followed by the final act of blowing up the balloons.I blew and blew,became redder and redder,then, exhausted, handed them to Grandad,who had roused from his nap and come to join us to do what I couldn't do.All the items were then stored in the front room ready for hanging on the next day,happy I journeyed to bed,Christmas Day was one day nearer.

****

"Slow and steady wins the race"

****

"Christmas is coming,Christmas is coming",I chanted as I left the school playground along with my friends,chattering noisily and excitedly,as we discussed what Christmas would have in store for each

of us.We ignored the chill of the fast approaching evening air,thoughts turned to the big day and myself and my friends were too excited to notice as we imagined what might be in our Christmas stockings.In a few weeks time we would return to school to see if my and all the others dreams had been fulfilled.The previous weeks had been taken up with the carol service and nativity play,the advent of Christmas had been a slow process.There had been a few clues as strangely shaped parcels had entered the house,only to be spirited away and hidden, but now with just five days to go the pace would become ever faster.Each year was the same, the festive preparation would be crammed into the last few days but this undoubtedly heightened the enjoyment for me.Years later when the day arrives the impact has been lost, it has just been spread out for too long.

Little signs,scarcely noticed,had in reality been appearing daily,signs so simple that I had almost missed them.Christmas cards began to be delivered soon after my birthday,mostly with Nativity scenes,Victorian scenes or the ubiquitous robin,which was always on at least one card.I would watch the thin,flimsy paper cards as they were removed from he white paper envelopes,themselves adorned by a Christmas Greetings sticker and stamp,excitedly waiting to see if it had any silver glitter on it.On occasions a parcel from a far off relative,far off being anywhere north of Fareham, would arrive,only to be smuggled away and hidden, with me being told "it's for Christmas Day and not before".As I made my way home I noticed the coloured lights appearing in some little shop windows,in the sweet shop in Lees Lane,"The Dugout", boxes of Milk Tray,Dairy Box,Paynes Chocolate Brazil nuts and pink,white and lilac coloured sugared almonds joined the everyday confections on the shelves.1956 was the first full year after sugar rationing and confectioners took full advantage,the pink and white sugar mice with string tails being a particular favourite,as were the gold and silver foil covered chocolate "coins".

****

"There are other fish in the sea"

****

Appearing from the fog laden gloom that was fast descending the man on his bicycle rode from lamp to lamp lighting the gas lights in Leesland Road,a long wooden pole reaching up to pull down the on off chain at the very top of the lamp.He whistled loudly,often out of tune the carol "Hark the Herald Angels" as he rode on his rounds."Not long till Father Christmas comes now" he shouted to me as he disappeared into the shadows turning into Norman Road."I know"I shouted back to him,"I wish it was tomorrow".Opposite Nana's in Leesland Road the piles of holly and evergreen lay on the ground outside of the two florists shops,the lights picking out the silhouettes of,Mrs Sands and Mrs Shepherd,respectively,cigarettes dangling from the corner of their mouths as they worked frantically almost feverishly,making holly wreaths for the coming weekend.They couldn't do them too early as the berries would drop off as they were only intertwined stems,with nowhere to store water in them,if they made them too late they wouldn't sell them all.The Sunday before Christmas I would accompany Nana to Ann's Hill cemetery with three of the finished wreaths to place on the family graves,a sign that although gone they were still remembered as part of the family.Christmas always brought family together,even those no longer with us.gone but never to be forgotten.Once indoors,a tea of hot buttered crumpets,toasted and

165

slightly blackened over the coal fire,I would then listen to Uncle Mac on the little bakelite valve radio hoping that it would be Dennis the Dachshund and Larry the Lamb with his characteristic phrase,"Pleeeze

Mister Mayor"Suddenly,from the end of the passageway,in the direction of the front door, floated the not always angelic airs of a Christmas carol "sung" by a motley crew,who were stood on the doorstep adding their contribution to the season festivities.A knock on the door as they finished,not always with the correct words,the shepherds apparently more occupied by socks than sheep,coupled often with an ascending"fueeel" at the end of their rendition of "Good King Wenceslas"was the point at which I would accompany Nana to the door carrying a teatray on which was lemonade,glasses and a plate of warm mince pies.A small monetary contribution for their efforts that may have ended up in a charity box but more often in their pockets so they could afford presents.Each little step added to the best time of the year and tomorrow I would accompany Nana on a few steps more of the Christmas journey.

****

"Through thick and thin,we'll get through it"

****

The rich fruit cake lay on the wire cooling rack and the air in the scullery was laden with smell of brandy that it was soaking up from the night before,the smell itself obscuring the odour of burnt milk from the over boiling porridge.It was Monday morning, back to Leesland School and today was the final rehearsals for the school Christmas events.At the beginning of December the roles for the traditional Nativity play had been decided,no volunteers,the "actors and actresses" were selected by our class teachers as to who they thought were the best candidates for the limited roles.every christian school in the land was preparing for the same events,ours was no exception as it was Church of England funded.Pupils were selected to play Mary,Joseph.the innkeeper,Magi and Shepherds,not forgetting the Archangel Gabriel and a supporting cast of various animals.The baby Jesus,in the form of a doll,made up the caste,everyone was hoping for a part but inevitably some would be disappointed and on the day of the performance would sit on the floor in front of the parents watching wistfully,turning to wave to a relative in the audience for reassurance,before they joined in the finale of'Away in a manger''sung by all..At this time of year I recall that everyday items took on new guises.Ribbons,bedsheets,tea towels and curtains,not to mention dressing gowns were to be seen in abundance in their alter egos of head dresses,cloaks and various other primitive items of clothing,our imagination knew no bounds.For the last weeks,when not learning my times tables or spellings I would be practising the lines for the play by repeating them over and over again,I mustn't get any wrong as I had been lucky enough to be selected for the part of a shepherd.The lines were few in number but I mustn't get them wrong as to me I was a star.In between all of this we would be learning the carols for the service at St Faiths Church which took place at the end of term.The assembled treble voices melodically performing the well loved carols,Oh Little Town of Bethlehem,Silent Night,Whilst Shepherds watched their flocks,Hark the Herald Angels Sing and Adeste Fideles,the church,on the day swathed in the warm glow of candlelight,the crib prominent in a prime position as you entered the building.I remember well the final play and the excitement and nerves,nobody wanted to make a mistake,the teachers final words"don't forget to speak up so the people at the back can hear"rang in our ears.The room full of proud parents and grandparents,umpteen rehearsals,thirty minutes,one performance and it was all over.I remember at carol service one of my friends singing a solo,eternally grateful that it wasn't me my eyes fixed permanently on Nana,who was in the congregation, as a source of inspiration and encouragement when we all had to join in.The religious element over until Christmas Eve and midnight mass,the last day of term at school was one of excited anticipation,shrill voices extolling their hopes and dreams for that wonderful day,in sight at last.The party atmosphere prevalent in every classroom,as each year had their own little celebration with simple snack food supplied by parents,with a little help from the teachers.The teachers were given cards and I remember a large purple Quality Street tin,decorated with the soldier and crinoline lady,as it passed round for each of us to take one sweet.Miss Dyer,Mrs Gamble,Miss Newnes,Mr Blackwell,Mr Boulind and Mr Washington would wish us a Happy Christmas as we left the classroom festivities,themselves relishing a well earned rest before returning in January to start a new year.

****

"Let a sleeping dog lie"
****

December the ninth was normally the anti climax before Christmas,I ould normally have a present,nothing expensive normally no more than ten shillings and a"special tea",comprising of meat or fish paste sandwiches,jelly,blancmange and an iced sponge cake and this year much was the same,it had passed uneventfully,after all it was really just another day,another birthday and another year.1954 had seen me experience real sadness,it had left an irreplaceable void in the family and Christmas certainly didn't have the excitement we normally had relished.Christmas without mum was empty,it would never be the same again but by the following year's event memories were hopefully not going to be quite so raw.I had started infants school and I had made new friends that I now went to school with.enabling me to join in and share the magic of Christmas with children as excited as I was.People I encountered were understanding and at times overly kind ,my friends parents I heard point out to their sons and daughters in whispered voices"that little boys got no mummy"or more poignantly on one occasion"how would you like it to have no mummy" I recall the December mornings when ice on the inside of window panes lasted all day,bitter winds cut you to the bone,the yellow smoggy air invaded your throat and made you cough,the only comfort the warmth of the cosy coal fires in rooms that at time filled with smoke.The "white"distempered walls and ceilings didn't look dirty until you went to repaint them and it was apparent the coal fire and Grandad's roll ups had taken their toll..As the month of December passed,at what seemed a snail's pace,my birthday each year heralded for me the start of the build up to Christmas..The next two weeks I experienced on a daily basis the events that would culminate in the greatest day of the year,a wonderland of magical inspiration,inspiration in itself which was so basic and so simple.Each little step added up to the final celebration,little things,a sheet of wrapping paper,a card,a packet of mixed fruit all were signs which meant Christmas was creeping closer.The cake,seemed to herald the beginning of it all,but in fact some things had been unwittingly prepared several weeks before.Pickles,chutneys and preserves had been prepared in October and "stir up Sunday" in late November saw the whole family giving the christmas pudding a stir before they made a wish.The phrase "stir up" not derived from the mixing but from a religious reference used at advent time.By mid December there was a change from this slow approach towards an unseen Christmas to a more frantic build up as both shops and shoppers realised there was only two short weeks left.Gradually,I remember items appearing in the shops like magic,all of them associated with this time of year and mostly unavailable at other periods of the year.The Co-op delivery man arrived on the

Tuesday with large stoned raisins,mixed candied peel,luscious glace cherries,green angelica and the little silver balls used to decorate the cake.All the ingredients were mixed together in a large ceramic bowl and I watched with anticipation as the mixed spices were added along with the currants,sultanas,raisins,eggs,flour,brown sugar and gravy browning and thoroughly mixed with a large wooden spoon.Gravy browning,was used to darken the colour of the cake and did not,strangely enough,taste even slightly of meat.Spooned into a greased cake tin lined with greaseproof paper,the remaining mixture in the bowl was dispatched into my ever expanding tummy,not quite sponge cake mix but it was sweet.As it baked the smell was mouthwatering,once cooked it would be left to cool on a baking wire, before a knitting needle was used to pierce the base at regular intervals prior to pouring a tablespoon or two of brandy over it.Left to cool overnight it would be wrapped in greaseproof paper then placed in an airtight tin in a the larder.It would be several days later that the marzipan and icing,being homemade of course,would be added to complete the task.Of course all of these luxury items didn't come cheaply,they had to be paid for and it was the culmination of a years planning,starting when the previous Christmas ended,coupled with thriftiness,that made it all possible.Every week of the year a small proportion of an already meagre pension,the married couples state pension was only two pound and two shillings per week,nowadays two pound and ten new pence,was put by for these luxuries,what you couldn't afford you didn't have.Co-op stamps purchased when paying the grocery bill every week paid for the cake ingredients,jellies,biscuits and such luxuries.Similarly the meat club at Mr Jones the butcher on the corner of Vernon Road provided the money for the extra meat enjoyed at Christmas,Dyer's Dairy in Whitworth Road had a club that paid for the cheese and cream and a ton time club,a savings club formed with the neighbours paid for the presents.and other little extras.Maybe only three or sixpence saved each week but it soon added up and ensured a good Christmas for those who could afford it.The school holidays were nearly here but before then there would be more excitement starting with the activities which started at school.

****

"You're getting your second wind"

****

Nana and I left my uncles at The Haven off of Clayhall Road,the weather pleasant enough as we headed in the direction of Haslar and Pneumonia Bridge.On the right a terrace of houses,on the left a brick wall topped with limestone coping stones making it too tall for me to see over.Approaching the maroon painted iron entrance gates that led into it I was able to see numerous marble gravestones that made up the memorials in the Royal Naval Cemetery.As Nana caught up I skipped to the end of the wall where there was a small grassy paddock and a ramshackle group of wood and corrugated tin sheds making up the buildings and sties of Baileys piggeries.In the pungent muddy puddles squealing black and white piglets played before joining the sow as she cooled off in the dirty straw awaiting Mr Bailey to return from his swill collection.People had no need to waste food if unwanted,highly unlikely,as there was rarely enough to eat,or if it was no longer edible,the pigs who were always hungry,would eat anything.The terraced houses became smaller in stature before being warfed by the wall that towered above them providing the boundary of Haslar Royal Naval Hospital,which had stood their from the mid eighteenth century.Built in 1753 the majestic buildings had many stories to tell of the incumbents,many who had spent their last days there, having returned from military campaigns around the world.Into sight came the gaunt grey and rusty structure of Pneumonia Bridge where we were able to cross Alver Creek and make our way down across the Trinity Green to the Gosport Ferry Office,a necessary destination as we needed to speak to Uncle Dennis,who worked at the ticket window.As we ran,or rather I ran,Nana, being less nimble,laden with bags,eventually caught up with me and I ran on to the other side.As I was running,the wooden ferry building in the distance my attention was drawn to something far more interesting.I stopped,I couldn't remember noticing it before but it wasn't an area I came too very often,the High Street was different we visited every week,but this was in a rather out of the way area.I stopped,as Nana approached saying to her"What's that" ,pointing to a rather ungainly craft which appeared to be just about to leave the muddy shoreline to what at this point was to me an unknown destination.The vessel was wide very flat,cumbersome with ramps either side which rested on the muddy beach,its funnels either side belched sooty smoke Its total appearance was one of decay as it slowly moved away carrying a handful of passengers,most with bicycles but there was one car.In a not exactly smooth manner it lurched accompanied by a worrying clanking and grinding noise which grew fainter as it made mid channel on its way across Portsmouth Harbour to dock close to the Camber Docks.Once there it would disembark its cargo and repeat the laborious exercise in reverse.Nana meanwhile was explaining to me that this was "the floating bridge or chain ferry"She explained that it had been crossing the harbour for over a hundred years and had once been very popular.It was a part of the Gosport ferry,but had become less used as it became more unreliable,we watched it safely arrive in Portsmouth as we walked along to the more orthodox ferry and at the wooden office met my uncle who was waiting to greet us.He and Nana exchanged words and then we parted company,he to ride home to Clayhall,me and Nana to get a number seven bus to Whitworth Road,just in time to miss the human caterpillar of Portsmouth Dockyard dockers invading the bus terminal.

****

"Two wrongs do not make a right"

****

March 1949 is possibly for me a significant date in my past, but was I there,maybe I was,maybe I wasn't but there is a strong possibility that that was around the time I started to develop, but I really can't remember.Whichever it was, it was now the reason that a small group of people were gathered,waiting in anticipation for the event about to occur in the bedroom of a tiny pebble dashed bungalow,entered by a dark green painted door,the top half of which had small square panes,this was 16 Oxford Road Gosport. As Christmas approached it promised to be a good one,a promise hopefully fulfilled but within five years the same bungalow was far more sombre in mood and the 9th of December 1949 was being viewed in a far less happy sentiment as it had in some way set the pattern for what took place a couple of months before my fifth birthday.On that day in 1949,although I didn't know them at that time, the people in attendance were Dr Mackenzie,a tall stooping man with wire rimmed glasses and neatly slicked back grey hair,a permanently smile dancing in his eyes.immaculately dressed in a grey suit.Next to him was a slight grey haired lady,of pensionable age, who was to be my Nana,Annie Brickwood,beside her was stood Nurse Skinner.A robust lady dressed in midwives uniform and for many years around that time and well into the 1950's could be seen pedalling furiously between home visits as she delivered her precious packages,her uniform flowing out behind her.She waved in acknowledgement as she hurtled pass,babies didn't wait so neither could she.Outside the bedroom door,impatiently waiting was my sister,was it to be a brother or sister,until I arrived nobody would know.The double bed in the small front room,in which the curtains were drawn,was occupied by a pale wan looking expectant mother,Violet Dewane[nee Brickwood],a trained dressmaker and seamstress by profession,she was awaiting the appearance of a little miracle,me.In due course I appeared,quiet at first,as I was tongue tied,but soon the silence was broken as a deft operation to rectify the problem by the medical expert on hand,the district midwife,was performed on the dressing table,putting matters to rights.Moving forward from this scenario that had been described to me by my Nana several years later it now moved to a time I do remember. It was now December 9th 1954, a day which I should have been anticipating with happiness,but this year was very different.I do remember that year and those first memories,which I recall,stemmed from the most devastating year I had experienced up to then.What had been from memory a happy early childhood,changed from late October that year affecting the whole course of my life.Audrey,my mum,had never really recovered from my arrival,she had often been unwell because of the heart condition she was living with,her health had gradually deteriorated,so contact with her had been necessarily limited.She had lain in her bed for much of the time,exhaustion and tiredness nearly an everyday side effect of her condition.Nana,who was getting no younger,worked tirelessly and was always there to help bring me up,along with my sister,so when mum was admitted to Guy's Hospital in London for a much needed operation we were hopeful that she would return to us with better prospects of improved health.That morning in October we kissed her goodbye and told her to hurry back,visits for the family would be difficult,the distance,road and speed of vehicles conspired to make it a whole day's journey and staying there was not an option as there was no money.We all watched her leaving in the white Bedford Commer ambulance,she weakly waved as she departed for what we all hoped was to be,for her,a life changing operation.Life changing,it was,but not in the manner any of us had anticipated on that day when she left.An agonising wait ended when the news arrived by means of a telegram a few days later that the pioneering heart operation had been a success,that she now needed rest and time to recuperate before returning to us waiting at home.Hopes were high when a few days later we were able to visit her at St Alban's Heart Hospital,over a hundred miles away,a whole day's journey.What started that day with an air of positive anticipation that we were to see her at last was the feeling she would be returning home soon,it helped to make the long journey bearable,later that day on our arrival home all was to turned upside down by the presence of a lone policeman,awaiting our arrival home,on the doorstep of 16 Oxford Road.These were the events that led up to me now finding myself on the Sunday before my fifth birthday,standing next to my Nana under a large cedar tree,beside a new shining white marble gravestone where we were placing fresh flowers.I knew why I was there but I had almost no clear memories of the person interred within,because of mum's illness contact when she was alive was limited.I remember the pink blancmange rabbit and red strawberry jelly.I don't remember any birthday party,there simply wasn't one,I do remember the white and blue iced homemade cake with its five candles,but nobody to help me blow them out.I don't remember Mum too well,although she wasn't there she wasn't far from our everyday thoughts,and Dad,well he wasn't there either,.he was always at work.To his credit he worked hard but it would have been nice to have him home more than he was,all I can think is that being at home was too painful for him. Birthdays were never celebrated,I often think Dad saw me as the cause of Mum's death but it doesn't matter 65 years later as Christmas is around the corner and I have some great memories to recount.Great memories of being around grandparents who in spite of very little money gave more than anyone could ever imagine,they gave their all,the love,the time,the effort that turned me into me.

****

"You are making much ado about nothing"

****

I would be woken at seven thirty every Sunday morning,summer or winter.I would wash dress in my best clothes,or my school uniform,comb my hair and light or dark,rain or shine would run down Rowner Lane to attend the eight o'clock communion service at the twelfth century church of St Mary the Virgin.It was less than five minutes away if I ran fast,passing under the lych gate,up the gravel path through the ancient gravestones I stepped down into the church and seated myself in a pew near the rear of the church.There were no other children there,but members of the congregation signalled their greeting and placing a hassock on the stone floor,I knelt to offer my supplication to the Lord.The organist started the service,hymns were sung communion was celebrated,I could not be a celebrant as I had not been confirmed but just played lip service.As we filed out of the church the vicar Reverend David Hawes,shook everyone's hand,the only other person to speak to me Lady Prideaux Brune whose family had been "the lords of the manor of Ruenore"from back in the time of the Domesday Book.She very kindly lent me her facsimile copy of the Domesday book entry which was her link with that past,she was keen to culture my interest in history by giving me the privilege of reading the ancient writing.

****

"Tell the truth and shame the devil"

****

The clocks had changed the month before,it was now November the change had brought darker evenings with it,I dreaded the impending cold,the choking,opaque,sulphur laden,yellow fogs and the damp air which invaded my throat and lungs.Tuberculosis was still rife at the time,the impending winter not a happy prospect for many,some who would not survive its freezing weather.Although fortunately not afflicted with the disease I did suffer with chest problems and uncomfortably every morning when I arose I had to be treated.The treatment was bizarre but common practice in those times.I was laid over a chair with a towel over my head to catch the steam from a bowl of steaming water.The idea was that the phlegm was loosened so that whilst I was thumped on the back I would be able to discharge it,into an accompanying chamber pot,whether it worked I can't recall but it certainly didn't do my back any good. As Bonfire Night had come and gone,my Guy burnt on the bonfire,my rockets launched and roman candles exhausted,I reflected on the celebration and I was not disappointed in any way.Unfortunately there was a price to pay,all the various combustibles had added to the sulphur laden smoke from the chimneys,which every house had so now laden with droplets of moisture the air made me cough even more in spite of a thick hand knitted scarf wrapped around my neck and face.After making my way home from Leesland School,there was little encouragement or inclination to venture outside again, once I was sat in front of the roaring coal fire,happily watching the bread threaded on the toasting fork take on the brown,sometimes black,of toast,before being smothered in butter and strawberry jam or golden syrup. Leesland Road was a quiet thoroughfare,traffic scarce even on a busy day apart from the No 6 Provincial bus,nearly always a single deck vehicle which ran once an hour in each direction.You were as likely to see a horse and cart delivering coal,wood,milk or vegetables or the rag and bone man collecting recycling materials as you were to see a motor vehicle.Often the quickest movement was Nana with a tin shovel and bucket rushing to retrieve the remains of the horses breakfast to fertilise the garden. Apart from when the bus disgorged its tired passengers as they returned from work,even then only a few,any other movement consisted of people walking or riding on badly lit bicycles.One of these bicycles arrived regularly,every evening and morning,that of the lamplighter who appeared out of the failing light to light or extinguish the gas lamps which were spaced at intervals along the length of the road.I say "spaced",although my memory is of no more than a half a dozen which emitted nothing more than a soft glow in their immediate vicinity. The nearest lampost to Nans,a cast iron affair with a lantern shaped top, was situated opposite the junction at the end of Norman Road providing nothing more than light to an area of just a few feet, really very little illumination,although it did provide a rather comforting feeling.

****

"Your life is what you make of it"

****

November saw the final leaves fall to the ground,leaving the branches of the trees looking like stark naked fingers pointing to the grey skies as summer had turned to autumn.As it did so the dream of Christmas,which seemed to have been so far away,for so long, began to take on a more positive feel.Today was Friday,no lessons till Monday and the next steps of Christmas preparation,the pickled onions,beetroot,red cabbage and chutney having been made in October, the turn of items with a shorter time in which they would keep we're about to be prepared.When Nana had been shopping the previous Thursday,in her basket she had placed additional items which she wouldn't normally purchase.She had now laid them out on the scullery table,to be added to after her visit to Mr Jones,the butcher,on Saturday morning.Most of the ingredients were readily available,found in most larders,but the journey to the High Street,with visits to the Maypole and Liptons,both grocery shops, had yielded tasty little extras,large raisins,which needed their stones removing,demerara sugar,candied peel and glace cherries.When Saturday arrived Nana and I made our way down to Whitworth Road to obtain the final required items.First stop of the day was,a visit to Mr Clogg's hardware shop,which saw us emerge a short time later with two large white pudding bowls and a roll of greaseproof paper.A visit to the butchers came next,we needed fresh suet and I watched as Mr Jones weighed it out and placed it in a paper bag.With only two more ingredients to purchase to complete our shopping list we returned back along Whitworth Road to The Junction tavern,the public house opposite Lees Lane railway crossing.With me waiting on the pavement,minors were not allowed in,Nana went through the door labelled the "bottle and jug",a euphemistic name for an off licence, before emerging with two bottles of stout,one for Grandad,and a miniature bottle of brandy which with the other bottle of stout was for the Christmas puddings.With the final ingredients now complete we were ready for "Stir up Sunday",the customary day in Advent when everyone stirred the Christmas pudding and made a wish,the name itself being adopted from the corruption of a collect recited in church at Advent,"stir up I beseech thee".After dinner on Sunday I helped to clear up,after which I helped fetch from the various shelves and cupboards all the bowls,spoons and utensils needed in the preparation of the pudding.Nana began by weighing out all the assembled ingredients,using a set of green scales with a steel tray,I then poured each one into a large ceramic mixing bowl,every so often she double checked the recipe in a little well worn green-blue covered notebook,although she had made these puddings many times before.In went the flour,fresh suet,stoned raisins which we had stoned the night before leaving to soak in brandy overnight ,sultanas and currants that had been soaked in cold tea,cherries,mixed peel,demerara sugar and grated carrot.Finally the brandy,which the raisins had soaked in,a tumbler of sherry and the bottle of stout was added and with a wooden spoon it was all mixed together,everyone in the vicinity suddenly appeared to help with the process,each making a wish as they did,Nana having told them of the event the previous week.We had been mixing most of the afternoon when someone mentioned that the mixture was unusually a little light in colour,it was that point that the mixing started all over again,although it had been with the other ingredients we had somehow failed to add the gravy browning,the item needed to darken the pudding.Finally evenly mixed it was time to spoon the mixture into the buttered white pudding basins before being covered with a greaseproof paper disc,the pudding cloth tied down and then the finished puddings placed in the copper to boil overnight,several hours later they would be removed,left to cool,then stored to mature in time for Christmas.The process had to be complete by the morning as Monday was wash day and the hot water in the copper was needed to do the washing not just to be discarded..

One thing however puzzled me at Christmas silver sixpences would come out of the pudding but I never ever remember putting them in but they must have been there,because there was pudding stuck to them!!

****

"A new broom sweeps clean"

****

When I visited the allotment or walked in the fields I learnt about the things that were constantly around me,how things grew,where meat came from,how milk was produced,where wool came from.Almost everyone in the course of their daily lives encountered farm animals of some type.It may have been chickens or ducks in a garden,rabbits used for meat,pigs in one of several piggeries situated in little semi rural areas situated amongst the houses.Horses pulled delivery carts and cows roamed the fields which broke up the small housing developments. Fifty years later,many allotments are now housing estates,the little town farms have vanished.larger farms are now more arable than livestock orientated,our familiarity with nature was what life was all about,life was appreciated and not wantonly destroyed.The following memory is only recent but rekindles and echoes the memory of nineteen fifty something when I was also five years old.Recently my five year old grandson came to tea and his favourite meal is sausages beans and chips.I loved sausages when I was his age but with mashed potato,peas and onion gravy,also my preferred sausage was a beef one but they don't seem to make them anymore even in the remaining butchers shops.Unfortunately we had no chips in the freezer
so I took him down to the bottom of the garden where I said we could get something to make chips with,he looked at me strangely but followed me anyway,stopping at the vegetable patch..When I put in the fork and lifted the large green plant revealing some potatoes he was

very impressed and on gathering them up and taking them indoors by turning them into chips he thought I was a magician.Once fried in the battered frying pan,on eating them he said to my wife "these chips are delicious".Never had he thought chips came from potatoes that were grown in the ground,but that they were in our very own garden was so exciting..As we had gone down the garden we had passed an extremely large white puffball growing in our copse and I explained to him that it was a fungus and showed him some more types, bracket fungus growing on a rotting tree stump along with "a fairy ring"which had sprung up in the lawn.A few days later on picking him up from school his teacher said " he has told us all about the footballs you grow in your garden but they have to be blown up"!! I stood slightly mystified and then it dawned on me "you mean the puffballs"I said as she smiled.It just proves a point that we had the knowledge and cared for the things around us,modern children have not had this chance and don't have that affinity with the natural world that we had,but that generation of ours now has the chance to rectify that.

****

"Don't be greedy,your eyes are bigger than your stomach"

****

Why I was walking down Stoke Road I don't recall but it was early evening,school had ended and I had been picked up by Nana and now I was walking past Erskine's garage and heading towards the town.It was the time of evening when it gradually became greyer and greyer,the time when the red pink shadows as the sun set were the only colour left in the sky.Lights were twinkling into life,the garage workshop in comparison was brightly lit,the little shops displayed chinks of light behind piled up window displays and windows obscured by advertising posters.I Walked past the Mocambo Coffee Bar,the pavement not yet littered with motorbikes,Bulls appeared on the corner,its hardware stock spilling onto the pavement,the huge red and white neon letters spelling out FORUM high up on the white front of the cinema,above the entrance canopy opposite.Where was I going,I just followed waiting for my companion to stop.eventually she looked over her shoulder and said "I'm just going in here",standing outside a rather uninteresting shop which appeared to sell jewellery.I however was taking little interest as the shop immediately next to it was Nobes toyshop,a far more interesting place so I said I would wait outside and look in the window.I turned towards the shop window joining other children already there,a little boy dressed in a grey raincoat and school cap,his sister with a straw hat and grey uniform,their eyes sparkled as they feasted on the scene in front of them.Standing next to them I sank to my knees,the cold pavement numbing my bare knees but it didn't matter,I gazed longingly at the treasures in the window."Father Christmas is ready" said a voice as the toyshop door opened,the little boy and his sister entered,it was obviously their mother who had spoken.Left alone on the pavement,above me an illuminated yellow sign in the window declaring Triang in red letters,I began longingly to look at the toys,buried beneath the cotton wool snow,silver and gold tinsel,sprigs of holly,striped Christmas stockings occasionally interrupted by a coloured light.The little train went round and round on its track,the black doll lay in her pushchair,Sooty and Sweep waited to sit on some childs hand.A toy umbrella,jigsaw puzzles of trains and animals,bats,balls,shuttlecock,ping pong balls diecast Dinky toy cars,a xylophone,drum set,recorder,board games were everywhere and I had started to daydream,I jumped as the door opened and the boy and girl came out with their rewards for seeing Father Christmas in his sparsely furnished grotto,sitting on his knee and telling him what they wished for for Christmas."Come on lad,let's get home" said a voice.

****

"What's sauce for the goose is sauce for the gander"

****

Early every morning including Christmas Day I would hear the chink of the glass milk bottles.They would be on the doorstep before I was out of bed the empty bottles removed at the same time to be returned to the dairy and washed,even though they would normally be sparkling from the efforts of the housewife,you were seen as "common" if you put out dirty bottles.Opening the door you were greeted with pint or half pint bottles,in the very early fifties the tops sealed with waxed cardboard discs.These tops had a hole in the middle which when they had been washed allowed my sister to make "pom-pom's"threading wool through them..By 1955 foil caps had replaced the cardboard for hygiene reasons,coming in two colours silver and gold.On summer ,mornings you would often be met by the sight of silver or gold shreds covering the doorstep,where blue tits had stripped the tops off the bottles to get to the cream,in the winter the tops would be perched an inch above the neck of the bottle supported by a plug of frozen milk.Through the clear glass of the bottle the thick creamy"top of the milk" was temptingly visible,the nearest we got to actual cream,if we were lucky we would have it on our porridge.Very often it would be saved and we would have some with tinned fruit or fruit tart on Sunday.If it had "turned"it would be used to make scones for Sunday tea,or shaken with some salt in a jar to make fresh butter.The friendly

184

rivalry of the Co-op milkman and the Dyers Dairy milkman as they met travelling in opposite directions down Leesland Road created many a laugh.The Co-op dairy being in Brockhurst Road and Dyers dairy being in Tribe Road.Both milkmen dressed in similar uniforms of white jackets with long leather apron,the black peaked caps they wore partially concealing the pencil tucked behind their ears,on collecting day a leather satchel slung over one shoulder and carrying a black ledger containing the bills they would knock your door for payment.Most people paid with aluminium milk checks,which they left under the empty milk bottles having purchased them from the dairy shop but money was just as acceptable.The days of dray horses were numbered and apart from Tom Parkers in Fareham the little electric hand carts now paved the way.The roundsman carried the milk in wire bottle holders,taking it from heavy wire crates.I remember Mr Weaver who lived at no 92,a tall man with tousled black hair going bald,he dressed in brown overalls and heavy black boots,he would arrive home from the dairy for his breakfast in a large red open sided articulated Co-op lorry with chains along the side holding in the crates of empty bottles or a stack of silver milk churns,His job was to collect the churns from the farm gates then,once processed,deliver the bottled milk to the distribution depots..Lost memories and how I do miss the top of that gold top milk,the nearest we came to having fresh cream.

****

"Everything is good for you in moderation"

****

Autumn was drifting into winter,October mists and grass sodden with dew were replaced with cold frosty mornings and the impending fogs fuelled by the smoke of numerous chimneys.With coal fires being the only real way to keep warm every house had at least one chimney and with fires in upstairs bedrooms more than often they had more. Bonfire night,on November the fifth, had burnt its way into the past once more, winter clothes,scarves,balaclavas,"long johns" and gloves had come out of mothballs,literally and we went around smelling of these and camphorated oil until the odour wore off,which could be weeks rather than days.Along with thick woollen socks inside our heavy winter shoes and rubber wellington boots we were ready for anything winter could throw at us,we even survived winters like that of 1962,weeks of snow when Portsmouth Harbour had thick ice in it and the sea froze at the edge of the beach at Stokes Bay.During half term,the week before the fifth of November we had been to Clarks shoe shop in Gosport High Street and this year had bought a new pair of shiny black lace-up shoes.One would have thought this would be a simple process but the measuring for length,width and leaving enough room for the foot to grow was a major exercise involving a footstool and a strange measure that was employed to get the correct dimensions.I was sure that the real reason was to try and part you from your hard earned cash in a time when most people were relatively short of money.We didn't have many pairs of new shoes,they were expensive, and very often they were worn till they were too small,pinched our toes and water entered through the holes in the soles,even lined with cardboard the water still came in.If they outlasted you then they would inevitably be recycled and a younger sibling,cousin or needy neighbours child would send them to the rag and bone man some time in the future.To make them last even longer,on the way home from the shoe shop we called in to the cobbler's shop,Mr Mills was the owner from whom we purchased four metal,kidney shaped protectors,which were nailed,they had several metal nails set in them,onto the toes and heels of the leather soles of the new shoes.This would be a task for Grandad,who would place the shoes on a cobbler's last,nearly every home had one,and hammer the plates into place. Once they were fitted,to the delight of the naughty children,who loved them,you could now slide far better on the paving stones on your way to school.On leaving the cobblers shop,with Mr Mills busy repairing shoes on a cluttered workbench,with the shop's interior poorly lit,and wearing a green visor to shield his eyes from the glare of a desk lamp illuminating his task in hand, we walked up Whitworth Road making our way home.As we progressed we made a detour to a little shop which was a delight to behold,a fair cornucopia of exciting as well as mundane treasures,owned by a reserved but extremely kind old man.Earlier that morning,stood on the doorstep at 80 Leesland Road,I had watched an elderly neighbour,from across the road,as he and his wife closed their front door before making their way down the road.Every morning at the same time they would follow the same routine,walking slowly, stick in hand the elderly man,wearing a built up boot due to his disability,arm in

arm with his wife made his way down the almost deserted road to open their shop which was next to The Junction public house in Whitworth Road and this was where we had now arrived.The tall stooped gentleman,always dressed in a black suit and white shirt,he had a long white beard,down to his chest, stained yellow from the pipe he smoked almost continuously, always looked deep in thought as if he was slightly troubled.His walk was purposeful,walking with the stick,which he raised in acknowledgement to any greeting coming his way,his shorter grey haired wife clutched his arm tightly. "Morning Mr Clogg,Mrs Clogg"would ring out and he would pause to raise his stick in the air.His shop was rather gloomy,dimly lit,but strangely inviting,the smoke from his pipe filtered out of the door,little room for it inside.On the pavement outside was an assortment of an ironmongers wares,tin baths,galvanised buckets,a simple single cylinder hand lawn mower,leant against the doorframe a stack of witches besom brooms,a popular item for brushing worm castes off of the lawn,gardening had now become a thriving hobby as the need for growing vegetables diminished and the garden became utilised for flowers and leisure time.As you advanced through the doorway you were greeted with metal dustpans,tin shovels,garden forks,shovels and the indispensable replacement wooden handles.These handles repaired brooms,mops,garden tools,hoes,prongs,spades and everything else that had a broken grip,repair was cheaper than replacement and the broken items were like "good friends" not to be deserted in their hour of need.Inside,the shop it was ill lit and full of dark corners,hiding many secrets,a passage ran down the right hand side,the wall,on this side covered in little wooden trays containing all manner of items,one of this,one of that.To the left was a long counter made up of lots of brass handled drawers,none labelled,but that didn't matter the vendor knew the contents off by heart.Behind this counter stood the bespectacled Mr Clogg with his black wire rimmed glasses perched on his nose,peering over the top off them as he waited for his customers,his wife nowhere to be seen.Each little drawer held its own treasures,each shelf on the wall behind him its own little gem.Hand tools were everywhere, tenon,bow and hacksaws chisels of various widths,handaxes,claw,sledge and pein hammers,screwdrivers,little oil cans,stood cheek by jowl alongside glass kilner jars,copper preserving pots and saucepans.Paper labels and wax paper tops for sealing jam jars,elastic bands,flat irons for heating on the fire or gas stove,a barrel of paraffin oil,waiting to be dispensed into customers jerry cans,putty with the aroma of linseed oil.In the drawers were no packets,just, loose iron nails,washers,nuts,bolts and brass and steel screws,various hooks,chains,candles bought by the pound weight,door latches,door bolts and the item we had come to buy,a roll of chicken wire which lay on the floor.The shop was as jumbled as this list,but everything had its place,Mr Clogg knew where it was, what that shop sold had no limits,sometimes it was just one of an item.hardware shops and ironmongers,where nothing was pre-packed,like this have now gone forever or maybe they are just waiting for a revival.

****

"All's well that ends well"

****

.

I remember Mr Horne,the grocer at the corner shop,as a short,slightly stout man with a jovial round face,flushed face,bushy white moustache and black rimmed glasses.He had a shiny balding head and wore a linen or white jacket with pockets either side. His wife wearing a flowery house coat also wore glasses and had permed greying hair swept up into a typical nineteen fifties style She wasn't much shorter than her husband but just as cheerful,it was obvious that she was the boss however.They would stock any groceries you asked for and although the little shop opened nine till five thirty every day,closed Sunday,half day Wednesday and Saturday on occasions a desperate customer could be seen knocking on the door to the house.In those instances they would smilingly obtain the required item telling the person,often a child,to come back and pay in the morning.Nothing was too much trouble the little shop was the focal point for the immediate local community and the hub of all local news,everyone trusted the owners which was a measure of their respect for the caring couple.I would often stand at the corner next to the shop as a delivery van unloaded and chatter incessantly to the driver and Mr Horne,probably to them a nuisance but if so neither showed their annoyance.

****

"Necessity is the mother of invention"

****

It's Sunday morning,I had reluctantly dragged myself from my slumbers,on opening the kitchen cupboards in the words of Old Mother Hubbard the cupboard was bare, there was no bread,no eggs in plastic cartons,no prunes,no bananas,certainly nothing for breakfast,but it didn't matter,I can get in the car and go to the convenience store,open all day,everyday,if I waited till ten o'clock we could go to the out of town superstore,have breakfast in their restaurant,then do the weeks shopping,the year is 2019,but things weren't always that way.So as I went to the driveway and got in the car I looked around to see how much my world had changed in sixty years,most houses still had their curtains drawn closed,there was no rush to get to church for the early morning communion service.As I drove to the local village it was seven thirty in the morning,I passed others hurrying home from night shift or to their day shift that was about to start, hurrying to take home that litre of milk that had once been delivered in pint glass bottles to the doorstep daily.Like the doorstep deliveries the little corner shops were heading in the same direction,wiped out by big impersonal retail companies.People shopping in the supermarkets,that sold almost everything,seven days a week,some open twenty four hours a day,but specialised in nothing even on a Sunday it opened its doors at ten o'clock.The church bells were silent,they either no longer were safe to ring,or were blamed for breaking the peace on Sunday by intolerant neighbours.The precise reason they existed,to summon the community to worship was no longer the priority it was almost of no significance, church attendances had dwindled,religion had lost its appeal.The two elderly ladies passing through the church lych gate,walking up the gravel path to the heavy oak church doors were a minority as they went to join the few worshippers already inside.On returning home,sitting eating my toast,made in a electric toaster I began to reflect on the changes which had taken place and how different it was from the 1950's.My first obvious thought was the peal of church bells and throngs of people making their way to church,all dressed in their Sunday best,they wanted to look their best in the Lord's house,they wouldn't entertain the thought of wearing trainers and tracksuits,to such a holy place,but where were they now.The shops no longer recognised the Lord's day,the day of rest,in the name of convenience"open all hours"was their strategy or was it just an excuse for people to be disorganised.They could buy what they wanted when they wanted,in spite of modern methods of keeping food fresh they purchased"on the day",or was it just greed or the pursuit of "the root of all evil",money, that was so important to them.One stop shopping had arguably reduced the freshness,very little produce was local,certainly the flavour of the food we were eating was inferior,it was just fresh because of the additives and preservatives pumped into it.In my childhood you would have visited lots of small shops,all of them staffed by knowledgeable experts,it took longer to shop but life was about living not just doing everything at breakneck speed.Bakers,butchers,dairymen,fishmongers,greengrocers,florist and grocers,they all readily imparted their expertise when asked and you could purchase in the quantity you needed as opposed to what you were forced to buy due to prepackaging.bananas,were a treat,vegetables were seasonal,fish was genuinely"the catch of the day"what the fishermen had landed that morning having been out all night.Cheeses were limited in their variety,nearly all home produced,made from locally produced milk.It was the grocers where probably you would see the biggest change,apart from less opening hours,most shops opened from Monday to Friday, nine till five thirty with an hour for lunch,from one till two.Saturday and Wednesday were half days so they were only open nine till one,and Sunday,nobody opened.it was God's day,the day of rest.I could run down to Mr and Mrs Hornes,on the corner of Leesland Road and Norman Road and watch enthralled,my nostrils filled by the variety of smells that accompanied the purchases.Vinegar could be bought in a jug,dispensed from a wooden barrel,ham on a stand would be carved by hand,bacon would be sliced from a side,of green or smoked,with a large red Berkel bacon slicer.Corned Beef,from a six pound Fray Bentos tin or a circular tin of Chopped Pork or Luncheon Meat would be sliced on a similar,but smaller slicer which varied the thickness of the slice by the turn of a dial.Sugar would be weighed from a large sack as would prunes,raisins,sultanas and currants,the fruity aroma of the dried fruit filling the air,nutmegs were to be grated not bought as powder Biscuits were displayed in glass topped square tins,sold either as broken biscuits or individual varieties weighed into paper bags in the quantity you wanted,a few ounces or a pound or more.Rice was sold loose,as were many other cereals and pulses,many items you could buy singly,you bought only what you wanted or could afford.I miss those days,yes.miss the convenience probably not,but maybe I would give even that up for the atmospheric shopping of the 1950's,as you went from shop to shop,the smells would waft around and everyone had a cheerful greeting and of course would say,"bye look forward to seeing you next week.

****

''A wise man keeps his own council''

****

It was much like any other autumn day,quiet,wet,dreary and generally uninspiring,there were still three days to go before the annual bonfire event.As was usual,waiting for a nine year old boy was not something that came easy,the bonfire had been built several days,sometimes weeks before,although it was constantly added to.Our fireworks had been purchased and stored on top of the bedroom wardrobe,out of my reach,the required refreshments for the big day on Wednesday,were stored safely in the scullery.With one eye on the weather and one on the state of the bonfire as it became damp my thoughts ran to what would happen if the fire wouldn't ignite.Eventually Sunday drew to a close and apart from viewing other bonfires as we made our way to Leesland School on Monday morning,noting whether they had been reduced in size by clandestine pilfering,there was little else to do except wait.The weather had been mostly dry in the ensuing days,although a few very heavy showers had made the bonfire a little suspect to whether it would ignite on the big day..The day seemed to never end,there were still two more to go,school lessons seemed to take twice as long as normal,excitement filled the air and on arriving home from school we could barely contain our impatience.By the time the day arrived I,like many children and their families found ourselves in the early evening heading towards the naval training base at HMS St Vincent in Forton Road,where we all enjoyed a spectacular public display before returning home to our own back garden display,or to attend a communal bonfire which had been assembled on a still empty bombsite,where an entertaining display could be enjoyed by all.On the parade ground,dwarfed by the tall rigged mast, tiers of wooden benches,the ground appearing clearly visible through the gaps between each row of seats,had been erected around the perimeter with its tall ships mast being the focal point. I climbed up the steps to the top row,where although several feet above the ground there was no rail to stop you falling over the back.Even more astounding,almost a daredevil scenario unfolded as in fact there were no safety harnesses either for the naval cadets who were manning the mast as a finale to the parade ground display.You held your heart in your mouth as the lads climbed up the mast in formation and out onto the side yardarms,the final boy,the button boy,standing at the very top on the smallest circular platform you will ever see.Lack of safety harness meant that a fall relied heavily on them hitting a large black cargo net stretched out at the bottom,with some degree of accuracy one hundred and ten feet below..The fireworks,in comparison to the ones we were to later set off at home were huge,green,blue and red rockets sailed into the sky,giant Roman Candles spewed out golden sparks and acrid smelling smoke pervaded the air.Suitably appreciated,a round of applause and the military band playing"God save the queen"the display finally over.The navy cadets safely back on terra firma,the crowds thronging out onto the pavement were occasionally accompanied by squeals of mixed fright and excitement as the odd mischief maker threw a jumping jack amongst the fleeing legs of the homebound crowd.Having hurried home,wrapped in woollen bobble hats,balaclavas,scarfs and gloves to protect them from the increasing damp and chill air,we enjoyed a hot cocoa before we returned outside.By now the bonfire was crowned with the guy,in some cases more than one if it was a community bonfire,taken from the shed where it had been stored.and now it was ready to be lit.the damp wood resisted doggedly to all attempts to ignite it,until,as if by magic,certainly with a scant regard for his own safety,although he did use a moderate amount of common sense,Grandad would empty copious quantities of paraffin oil onto the wood and paper.Walking around the fire,leaning forward,striking a match,then swiftly stepping back,it was lit in a number of places,as it burnt and the ashes built up,potatoes in their jackets and recently collected sweet chestnuts were placed unwrapped into the glowing embers.Whilst the fire began to sink and settle into a hot glowing mound,mugs of hot tomato soup appeared from Nana's kitchen to warm us inside,the bonfire performing the same task warming us on the outside.Blackened jacket potatoes,now well cooked were removed gingerly from the ashes,cut open and butter added before we gnawed our way through them,"a little ash never harmed anyone" we were told.Hunger satiated it was now time to watch the fireworks."Stand back",we were instructed,as we huddled in a group stamping our feet.our hands tucked in our armpits to keep warm,some even watching through the curtained window from indoors,it was so damp and cold.As Grandad scurried back and forth.In between the larger fireworks we would be handed coloured matches burning green and red or giant sparklers which,as they finished,we threw into the air to watch the stream of sparks as they fizzled out.Spinning Catherine wheels flew through the air having escaped from the pins securing them to a tree trunk or wooden post,rockets collided with the wall as the glass milk bottle fell over and Mount Vesuvius and Sparkling Leaves roman candles toppled over and provided an unwelcome display to the unfortunate worms.Grandad,meanwhile thought he was back in World War 1 and spent his time frantically attempting to escape the self produced bombardment,by hiding in the shed,all in all it was close to a disaster,but we all survived.At last as the chill,damp air became filled more and more with swirling acrid,gunpowder laden smoke from the many fires and projectiles that had crossed the sky,the bonfire was checked to see it would present no further danger as it was now time for bed.The one night a year celebration was over again,the following morning the milkman on his rounds cursed the sooty milk bottles which he was now collecting.They had launched numerous rockets the night before but would never be used for milk again.The school children on their way to school searched for and collected the spent rocket sticks,looking for spent fireworks but for what use or reason none of us really knew.We had fifty days to wait now,in my case only thirty four,before the next exciting event of the year,for most children. Christmas for most,for me a birthday, but both anniversaries were well worth the wait.

****

"All things come to he who waits"

****

Every weekend the highlight would be the traditional Sunday Roast dinner,which influenced to a great extent what we ate for the rest of the week.Meat was expensive so the amount of meat on your plate at mealtimes was necessarily small,one or two slices at Sunday lunchtime would be the most an adult could expect as a child it would be one thin slice.However it didn't matter,there were plenty of potatoes and seasonal vegetables from grandads family allotment that had been kept going even after the end of the war.It was always meat and two veg,the seasons dictating what was available,the variety was far less than you would imagine,cabbage,peas,runner beans,carrots and swede tended to make up the bulk of the meals.Yorkshire pudding was a good fill up,but only if we had beef,thick gravy made in the roasting pan with the meat juices added flavour but we didn't have Yorkshire pudding if we had lamb pork or the occasional chicken.Sage and onion stuffing would only accompany poultry,mint,apple,or horseradish sauce served with lamb,pork or beef respectively.Cold Yorkshire pudding,on roast beef days, may well be served when cold spread with jam as a "pudding"..Inevitably the joint was purchased with the bone in it,to add flavour we were told,having had it cold on Monday,minced in cottage pie on Tuesday, on Wednesday with very little meat left on them the bones were consigned to the simmering stew pot.Dumplings,made with suet to fill you up were added to eke out the meal,the meat having been only what had been left on the bones and it wasn't usually a great deal.The bones were always dished up with the stew ensuring no meat was wasted,if it had been a chicken at the weekend the feet would have been scrubbed and added as were the giblets and neck.When the chicken stew was served we waited with bated breath to see who would get the wishbone,then with your neighbour at the table we would hook our little fingers around each branch of it and pull.Whoever ended up with the large piece where the two arms met could then make a wish,careful not to say what it was as if you did it wouldn't come true.I wondered how many did,similar number to those that we made when we saw a rainbow I expect,simple things but they made us happy in days of simple,uncomplicated lives.

****

"Has the cat got your tongue"

****

It was the end of half term week, it had been a week of inclement weather bringing cold and damp and Saturday was the last chance for me and all my school friends to make the final preparations.If everything wasn't organised and completely ready by Saturday evening it would be too late,Sunday was church day and next week we were back to school so I was up early as most of the day would be spent scouring gardens,yards and anywhere that we might find some pieces of wood.Rising early,the darkness hid the damp,but at least it was not rainy day,so after a warming bowl of porridge I made my way to the old garden shed to retrieve my trusty pale blue,now battered pushchair.It had served my sister and I well as small children but had ow been relegated to its present resting place a few years before,at almost twenty years old it was relegated to transporting combustible items to the ever growing bonfire situated on the still undeveloped bomb site further down Leesland Road.Meeting my friends along the road,we sullied forth,as did several others from rival bonfires,the competition was fierce,we all wanted the best bonfire in the neighbourhood and collecting wood,in fact anything that would burn was important, but not the only activity that took place that day.At dinner time we split up to go for our midday meals and when we reconvened an hour or so later the pushchair now had a passenger,it now carried the crowning glory of the bonfire,the guy,ready to earn his keep before being burnt.We decided where we were to go after a brief discussion,was it to be The Junction,at the corner of Whitworth Road and Leesland Road, or in the opposite direction from no eighty,The Foresters Arms at the corner of Anns Hill road and Leesland Road,both suitable sites for the task we had planned.The second mentioned public house had once been where my maternal great grandfather,Alfred Brickwood,had reigned as the landlord at the turn of the twentieth century after his retirement from the Royal Artillery.The Junction was the preferred destination,however,as it was near a bus

198

stop and far busier and we needed a lot of people to achieve our objective.Accompanied by our effigy of Guy Fawkes in the trusty pushchair,we made our way to the elected hostelry to happily find we were the only guy there,immediately a good sign,no competition.This could be a propitious time as several over indulged individuals,unable to differentiate the coins in their pockets,would mistakenly impart a half crown or florin in error,a copper or two being the more usual expected donation..As the premises closed at two thirty we hurriedly made our way home to count the spoils and add the new sum to the previous days collection.Not all the collection was used for fireworks as I would retain some for the purchase of Christmas presents later in the year,it was not right to let all that money"go up in smoke",especially when money was so tight.The guy was placed in a chair in the living room,a final luxury before his demise on the big day,he had become to me part of the family,the pushchair was returned back to its dark corner at the back of the shed,its eventual resting place I can't recall,but I feel the rag and bone man played a part.

As Saturday evening fell I would make my way down with Nana to the local newsagents in Whitworth Road in order to obtain a late final copy,printed on bluish paper,of the Portsmouth Evening News.This gave us the chance to catch up with all the local football scores and allow dad and grandad to check their football coupons.Nearly every male member of a household filled in the football coupons from Vernons or Littlewoods,which were collected from the doorstep every week.They were also available at many newsagents along with those from a smaller company called Zetters,it gave ordinary folk the chance to wager a few pence per line,eight draws promising the prospect of a life changing sum of money.This Saturday evening,unlike most however,the trip also had another purpose and the spring in my step was due to that purpose.It was time to select and buy our chosen fireworks,using the collected money, for the great night of November the Fifth,the array of various types was limited,but nonetheless it was an exciting time.fireworks were mostly purchased singly,sold from a large locked box behind the shop counter and actually chosen from a picture chart on top of the counter..Once the choice was made they would take them from the locked box and hand them to you in a brown paper bag with the rocket sticks projecting from the end.Although selection boxes were available,most were sold loose,there were standard and giant sparklers sold in white paper sleeves and red and green coloured matches wrapped in a piece of newspaper inside the matchbox.The main manufacturers were British being,Astra,Brocks and Standard,the fireworks only on sale for a week before the day and never on sale after the fifth of November.They were only set off on that one traditional evening,never before or after,any used before or after that day saw a visit from the local "bobby" and almost certainly t least a fine,zero tolerance was the accepted normal.They were nearly all ignited in the limits of small family celebrations or a communal bonfire supervised rigidly by local parents,there were just a small number of organised displays such as the one organised by the Royal Navy at HMS St Vincent.The fireworks which were selected from the large colourful pictorial chart,were each   marked with the individual price,allowing us to add our purchases as we selected them,mental arithmetic being a skill of the times.There were Roman Candles,Mount Vesuvius,Mount Etna,the same firework except one was green and one red,Penny Bangers,Thunderflashes,wonderfully scary Jumping Jacks,Catherine Wheels,Rockets and giant Sparklers.In packets of six or twelve sometimes red or green,they were either small ordinary items or large monsters,about twelve inches long,whichever size they were all sold in the same white sleeves with blue printing.Matchboxes with matches,large brown heads with green or red tips which when struck flared up in the colour of the tops,we bought them all,or at least as many as our money would allow us.Money exhausted we wandered home where Nana or Grandad,who had carried the fireworks,me not being allowed to,either took the fireworks upstairs to put on top of the wardrobe or to the shed,placing them up high out of reach in the expectation that they wouldn't be touched or talked about until the evening's parties were ready to begin.

Nobody let fireworks off on a Sunday,it was not only a religious day but illegal,even if Bonfire Night fell on that day it would normally be carried over to be held on the Monday night,interestingly never the night before on Saturday,a little longer wait for us to anticipate the display that we had purchased.The excitement of that display,the frustration of waiting a little longer,worse still another day at school,a day which felt it had more hours in than normal.

****

"You get nought for ought"

****

I had been aware for some time that languishing in one corner, of Nana's rickety garden shed,stood an old pale blue pushchair which had seen many better days.It had spent most of the last fourteen years transporting my sister and then me on a daily journey from Leesland Road to Oxford Road,as well as undertaking other various journeys when it was loaded with toys,clothes, food and drink on a day out,its usefulness now outgrown it just stood gathering dust,until now.Once more it had become sought after,an item of usefulness before it finally departed forever,not for its function of transporting children exactly,but now it was just what I needed to transport things that to me were just as important.Digging it out from under the empty hessian and net sacks which were piled on top of it,sweeping away the thick cobwebs and dust avoiding the large black garden spiders it finally came into full view.

As I pulled it squeaking and creaking out into the backyard I was greeted with "what are you doing with that,I don't want that dirty thing brought indoors what do you want it for, it's ready for the rag and bone man". Nana was right,it was,but not before I had pressed it into service for this one last time to perform a task far more important than carrying me and my sister around the streets of Gosport.Grudgingly I started to clean,I hadn't anticipated the need of using a bucket of warm water.I fetched the bucket of clean water from the kitchen,taking no time at all to turn it a muddy brown,then using a small oil can I lubricated the axles of the white tyred wheels before laying sheets of old newspaper on the floor in the house,to catch any oil or remaining grime that might drip or fall off as I pushed it through the kitchen and living room, down the passageway and out of the front door.It was the last week of October and I was in a hurry,time was short as in ten days time it would all be over for yet another year.A couple of pals joined me,so with a "just going out Nan,not going far" I joined forces with them and pushchair to hand we started to go on our scavenging hunt.We made our way down the road to the shops at Whitworth Road and Lees Lane crossing,when we arrived we timidly entered them one by one,some we came out of empty handed but others were more fruitful in our search.Mr Clogg was always a ready donor,such a nice humble gentleman,always ready to give some old wood and even a half a crown towards the fireworks.The newsagents gave us some old cardboard,no papers as the unsold ones were returned to the wholesaler and credited to the shop the following day. Returning through Harcourt Road we clambered over the wall of the old Ann's Hill Cemetery looking for fallen branches from the old fir trees that grew along its boundary with Leesland Road and then went around the back alley ways checking every hiding place we could imagine before returning home with whatever bonfire fuel we had managed to collect.Once we had manoeuvred the pushchair back through Tribe Road,by now fairly well laden, we crossed over to the bomb site where the bonfire had grown several feet higher from mostly garden waste,as we passed we looked longingly but our destination was our own modest affair in our back garden.We cut down Norman Road and manoeuvred the pushchair and its load down the narrow alleyway that ran between the back gardens of Leesland Road and Norman Road.There was no back entrance to the garden of Nana's house so we had to throw the contents of the pushchair over a low brick wall,in itself not an easy task because of the"conker" tree which stood in the corner of the narrow garden.We piled the branches over the wall,which my friends climbed over, whilst I walked back around to the front door,negotiated the passageway with the pushchair and met them

back in the garden to assist in adding to our little bonfire.It stood on a patch of soil at the end of the back garden,far enough away from the chicken run to avoid roasting them alive.It was only small,but it was a start and by the end of half term it would be as huge as the garden would safely allow,which really wasn't huge at all.Happy that we had made a start,we split up for dinner and met up just after one o'clock to prepare for the next step of our plan.The next step also involved the use of the pushchair,once more,for a task more in keeping with the purpose of it,as a conveyance for an occupant too tired,or unable,to walk.After dinner saw us constructing this passenger,although it had not been known for a mischievous little boy to be used as a substitute at times.Old socks,old trousers,old shirt,old stockings,an old cap,string and the most important item old newspapers.Having removed all the buttons,to the button tin,we tied string around the legs and sleeves of the old clothes and then proceeded to stuff newspaper in,resulting with us,once assembled,of giving it the semblance of a figure.As a last resort if we hadn't made enough money earlier in the week from running errands a circle of cardboard,cut from an old Kellogg's cornflake packet had a face drawn on it and now we had a "Guy",On most occasions the cut out wasn't needed as a few days earlier we would have had enough money to be able to purchase a proper "moulded.painted face Mask"when we had accompanied Nana to the paper shop to pay for the news bill.Suitably tired we went to bed,the anticipated excitement of the coming days preventing us from falling asleep until we could fight no longer and drifted off to our dreams.Guy ready,time to kill,"idle hands do the devils work"and the work we had planned was mischievousness at its best.My friends and I had retained some money we had collected and persuaded an accommodating elder to purchase a box of penny bangers,not for bonfire night, but to play some tricks.We had tried unsuccessfully to make fireworks with ground match heads,copper sulphate and iron filings but didn't achieve a great deal.With the illicit bangers however Iwas able to blow Airfix planes,well watch them melt and one or two bangers in the guy on the bonfire was very uplifting.

****

"Birds of a feather flock together"

****

The watery sun heralded damp pavements and there was a distinct chill in the air,but come what may nothing was going to prevent today from happening.Gulping my breakfast down,much to the annoyance of Nana who reminded me"to mind my manners and not to eat with my mouth open" not to mention "to chew each mouthful one hundred times" most people still weren't about,when groaning I emerged from the doorway with a tin in one hand after I had dragged the laden pushchair,complete with Guy,through the house to the front doorstep.A cardboard sign I had made saying "penny for the guy" was propped up on the battered pushchair and I waited and waited,there was very little movement and the passers by that I did see were on bicycles.I wasn't he most patient of children so I relocated to Hornes corner shop hoping people might drop a copper or two into the tin from their change from their shopping.The roads were quiet,apart from residents

popping to the shop,all of them in a hurry,by lunchtime I had collected only one or two coppers only one or two people had passed and the anticipation of the morning had not been fulfilled. Once we had that proper mask,things would improve I told myself and rather than sit outside Horne's shop on the corner of Norman Road,as the week continued we made our way further afield,sitting outside The Junction or Forester's Arms public houses,often several different guys vying for their share of the spoils.I soon learnt that you had to be the only "beggar" at a location as people were short of resources and even a penny was a lot of money to many people and unaffordable as a gift.Begging was not an acceptable behaviour,but Guy Fawkes night with it's "Remember,remember the fifth of November" nursery rhyme was an exception to the rule,similar to carol singing at Christmas and the boy scouts "bob a job" at Easter..Fireworks were sold for just one week before the actual day,a simple tradition adding pleasure after the austerity of the war years,in a time before progress that gave a lot of pleasure on one night.

****

"Speak when you are spoken to"

205

Slowly the sunny summer mornings started to fade,replaced by mists hat lingered longer in the autumnal mornings,dampness started to fill the air and dew lay heavy on the grassy fields.As the blackberries disappeared,eaten by both birds,animals and people they were replaced by field mushrooms,inedible fungi and toadstools,following on from them hazelnuts chestnuts and walnuts were ready to be picked and stored for use later in the year.At this time of year mist and fog started to remain all day and evenings were uninviting,the freshness of the early morning mists were replaced at the end of the day by cold air laden with a yellowy smog,dampness everywhere, swirling under the gas lamps in the road.I would wait for the number 6 bus to arrive at the bus stop in Leesland Road at its junction with Norman Road,an inviting warm golden glow announcing its arrival as it came closer through the smog to carry me home.These clinging fogs were constantly fuelled by the sulphur and nitrogen laden smoke which poured from every chimney crowning the roofs of the Victorian terraced houses,its choking presence a necessity if we were to keep warm.As October moved to a conclusion it was time to harvest the last fruits from the trees to store for winter most of these being apples and pears Cox's Orange Pippin,the pips rattling inside signalling they were ripe,alongside Charles Ross,James Grieve,Egremont Russet,Lord Lambourn,all following on from the earlier rosy red Discovery apples which were not suitable to store over the winter.To leave them any longer risked losing them,any blemished or bruised fruit taken for immediate use,the perfect fruit carefully dried and polished before being individually wrapped in newspaper or sometimes dry sand and stored in wooden crates,which were then placed in the cool of the garden shed to keep for Christmas,a similar treatment befalling the hard Conference pears,which rarely ripened on the tree.Whilst all of this was taking place the trees would receive their yearly haircut, the need for this annual treatment had meant nearly all everyday folk knew how to prune their fruit trees and bushes.Up at Middlecroft Lane,on his allotment Grandad would have a pile of green twigs,too small to burn on the home fire,not suitable for compost,so with a pile of damp leaves he would simply add to the smoke laden air.With fondness,I could watch the white wispy smoke ethereally rising from the smouldering bonfire,as it rose from the leaves,the smell of the green applewood was deliciously autumnal,a smell found nowhere else.In the little gardens at the rear of the terraced houses,nearly everyone had at least an apple tree,the piles of prunings from these used to be added to all the pieces of scrap wood that we had been collecting all month preparing for the next momentous occasion,November the fifth,Bonfire Night.Autumn was well and truly here,winter was not far behind and the first frosts often arrived before the clocks changed at the end of October.

****

''A penny for your thoughts''

****

The summer evenings had almost faded,the evenings slowly but surely were drawing in and we had already started to prepare for the icy cold winter that almost certainly would soon be with us.It had been a long hot summer and as the hedgerows were laden with hips,haws,holly berries and bramble an extremely hard winter was predictably in store if we were to believe the folklore of the time..As John Keats had written in his "Ode to Autumn" it was "the season of mist and mellow fruitfulness".and for us the opportunity to share some of it with the rest of the countryside.We were privileged as dad had a car supplied by his company,a blue and white Hillman Minx which we would use to take trips out at the weekend in order to enjoy the various hedgerows, woodlands, copses,fields,commons and streams that were fresh,clean and unspoilt.Goodwood was always a favourite.Earlier in the summer the climb up The Trundle,through the wild orchids growing on the chalk slopes,rewarded you with views out to the Solent,then looking back you viewed the horse racing course in all its majesty.The Edwardian Cafe along Fairmile Bottom,which closed for the winter months,was a timber building where the charabanc trips from London to Bognor Regis stopped over for refreshments,a cup of tea,a scone,a piece of cake or ice cream.All around the tearooms stood Slindon Forest where,once in amongst the ancient trees we would gather plump sweet chestnuts,ready to store and roast over the open fire at Christmas.In nearby thickets we would collect hazelnuts from the coppices which edged the chalk sward,careful not to pick the ones with neat holes drilled through the shell by a marauding grub,you picked the brown nuts that separated easily from the little "fairy hats" that held them secure.Nearby the oak would shed acorns from their stippled "fairy pipes".whilst in the hedgerows "robin's pincushions",fiery red,would adorn wild dog rose bushes,hidden amongst the red rose hips,the same rose hips that gave us our itching powder.In the same way as the oak apples,minus their little wasps,would appear under the oak trees,nearby copper beech trees began turning colour as they dropped their mast in the forest,in years before providing pannage for the pigs which grazed beneath them.I often wondered if the little yellow and green packets of Beech Nut chewing gum that we bought from machines attached to shop walls had any connection.Dry dead tree branches we came across would be collected,somehow fitted into the already bursting car boot and its load of picnic necessities,before being brought home in the car.If the car boot was empty enough dad often filled hemp sacks.he had brought with him,with rich dark leaf mould from the forest floor a cheap source of soil enrichment.Firewood was always welcome wherever we went if they had been collected from the local cemetery they would have been dragged slowly along the pavement,all welcome extras for the winter fires

****

"It takes one to know one"

****

This was the time of year when the first mists used to hover above the fallow fields,at Titchfield Haven the fallow deer,appeared as ghostly outlines grazing on the remnants of this year's harvested crops,the harvest long gathered in,joining them from the sky skeins of geese flew in to get their share.As we rode our bikes through the shadowy mist there were shadows all around,sometimes a poorly lit car,heard but not seen would appear like a spectre as it crawled along,the driver peering intently through a screen that was almost obscure,.As Michaelmas approached,the little purple daisies of the same name were visible in many gardens,their leaves covered in a coating of white powdery mildew,soon harvest would be celebrated,no signs of the pagan celebration of Halloween.Such a non christian festival involving the devil was not welcome at a time when superstition dictated that if you spill salt you would throw a little over your left shoulder"to blind the devil,throwing even the smallest piece of food in the fire was seen"as feeding the devil"and pumpkins were still in America.One seed however which provided the most enjoyment to me,as a little boy,was the horse chestnut,the humble conker which provided hours of untold fun.At Leesland School or nearby in leafy Green Lane there were lofty horse chestnut trees,which spilt their conkers onto the paths or pavements,normally however not quickly enough for me and my friends.Shoes,plimsolls.school bags sticks,in fact anything we could lay our hands on was hurled into the branches for me and my friends to dislodge the prickly green cases.Once gathered from the ground they accompanied us home to be prepared for the battles that would soon arrive.They were baked in the oven and pickled in vinegar to harden them for combat,before using a meat skewer to make a hole through the nut,also your finger at times,once string was threaded through and knotted we were ready,cheating a little but ready. Holding the conker up high your opponent would aim at your conker with theirs,if you moved yours and they missed hitting yours they would have a second shot.Your turn came next,the aim being to destroy your opponents conker before they destroyed yours.If you won you would be the proud owner of a "oncer",if the one you had been beaten had already won a "fight" it would be a "twicer" and so it went with "forty niners"and such.Grand days,great fun but just around the corner the fun was going to start with a BANG!

****

''You can't have your cake and eat it too''

****

"Memory Lane" the cake boxes lay waiting to be opened,the delights inside cried out to be eaten,and whilst doing so my day dream began....Memory lane came in many flavours and each one led to many different places,there was no definitive destination as all the journeys were in my own mind.now,many years later we have superstores,retail parks and large department stores but "Memory Lane" is still there to spin the magic to rekindle the memories made by those original cakes in the nineteen fifties.All the specialist shops have disappeared,but when I see those words on a cake box each cake transports me back to the missing links and jobs no longer there,what I as doing when eating that particular cake.I watched as Mr Shephard and Mr Stanley led their horse and carts along the road,the milkman had been up at dawn with his horse drawn milk float.None needed to tell their equine charges where to stop the horses knew their customers and where to stop,where they would get a carrot or apple treat.The rag and bone man collecting recyclable items in his handcart,the knife sharpener with his bicycle,putting his bike on a stand,his pedalling drove the millstone to sharpen knives,shears and scissors.The Romanies with their wooden clothes pegs,the gypsies hawking white heather,offering to tell your fortune if'you crossed their palm with silver",now all gone.The coal man carrying his hundredweight sacks on his shoulder,the hawker or tinker selling his trinkets offering to repair pots and pans..I'm still stood on the doorstep,a slice of "Grannies Farmhouse Fruit cake,with its sugar crystals on the top,now hardly able to understand how we have lost all these jobs,once so important to our existence.Crumbs falling down the front of my jumper I walked along a now, empty road,the little shops which had inhabited every corner had turned back once more into houses.The terrace of shops in Whitworth Road had no dairy.no ironmonger,no butcher,no cobbler at his last.The little wool shop gone as was the sweet shop,and also the tobacconist.The greengrocer,the baker even the paper shop with its paper boys was disappearing into the past.Passing a small builders yard hidden behind tall blue wooden gates,the joiner,carpenter and plumber making their window frames,doors and lead pipes from basic materials were redundant,everything being prefabricated,their skills fast disappearing.So many jobs,so many skills,so many trades lost for ever,and even in the countryside jobs were vanishing.No hand milking or herdsman,no pigman,few shepherds,no ditchers,no hedge layers no carters or wagoners in fact very few farm workers,very few livestock farms.

At Brickwoods brewery,on The Hard in Portsmouth you could see a cooper making his wooden barrels ably assisted by a muscled blacksmith, who would also shoe the horses for the carter,responsible for the provision of shires for the drayman.Even at the end of life the coffin maker and gravedigger have been replaced by mechanisation,cake eaten it was time to throw the box away and like these jobs. It became just a memory in Memory Lane.

****

"There are storm clouds on the horizon"

****

The clouds began to redden,as the coppery tones of the sun began to spread its fingers across the morning sky dispersing any lingering mist,which filled in the furrows of the fallow brown field.The harvest had been gathered in,all that remained was a few areas of stubble the stooks which had been stacked in the field were now straw bales in the barns,the heads of corn stored in the granary,stood on its steddles.We had harvest thanksgiving festival to look forward to,one of my favourite times of the year.As we walked along the field edge,dog running alongside we looked at the wildfowl taking off from Titchfield Haven making their way to their feeding sites.The sack we were carrying was filling out as I gleaned the wayward corn stalks at the edge of the field.The corn would go to the chicken in Nanas back garden,the straw stalks provide bedding for the rabbit in its hutch in the backyard.

****

''If ifs and ands were pots and pans there would be no need for tinkers''

****

Early Saturday morning,but chilly as it was,Dad and me,walked up Oxford Road,across Southcroft Road before walking through the little alleyway opposite leading to Mill Lane which ran along the back of the bungalows in Southcroft Road.Following the path round to the right towards Privet Park,our golden retriever close behind,we passed the site of the fatal helicopter crash which had occurred a few weeks before coming to a left turn taking us past the allotments on one side and the Royal Navy playing fields on the other.Arriving at the park we entered the park through a gap in the hedge,the mist still hung over the dewy sward,but amazingly there in front of us in little white patches was breakfast! Why they grew there I know not,but dad would come every year for a short space of time for those wild mushrooms.Only small,very few at a time but to this day their flavour has never been surpassed.Having filled our pockets we hurried home the way we had come,once back home the frying pan appeared and in no time a breakfast of bacon,egg,sausage and mushrooms was sat on the table waiting to be eaten.After breakfast my day was spent at Nana's,dad having to work Saturday mornings and if Portsmouth were playing football at Fratton Park in the afternoon he would be found there.This time of year saw winter preparations begin and today was to be the first delivery of fuel for the winter heating.Mr Stanley with his horse and cart delivered our log supply in wicker baskets,the smell of the damp newly chopped wood had a smell of its own which is still in my memory.Mr Blundell, the coal man would carry hundredweight sacks on his back,through the house before emptying them into the avaricious mouth of the coal shed.Whilst this was taking place my Saturday morning was spent making much needed firelighters to store for winter.Made of several sheets of newspaper folded into a long strip then by twisting it alternately you arrived at a rigid structure,something loosely resembling a spring which was long burning.Empty Kellogg's cornflake packets were cut down to the size of a brick and then filled with a mix of cement dust and last years coal dust.Emptied from the coal shed prior to the delivery and added to the cement dust when mixed with water to the consistency of porridge and poured into the "mould" it was left to harden. When the weather became too inclement and coal was at a premium these homemade briquettes were used as a supplement.

****

"Every dog has his day"

****

The weather on the Sunday proved to be fine so after the regular visit to the cemetery at Ann's Hill to replace the flowers we arrived back home carrying several small branches,fallen from the old trees,to be added to the fuel store.After dinner,with summer fast approaching its end, we would make use of the fine day and head,by car,to the downs at Goodwood.The woods in that part of the country,which bordered the edge of the downs,held a bounty of riches.Along by the racecourse car park area there were thickets of hazel trees where we picked cobnuts to be dried in the oven when we arrived at home.The hedgerows were giving up their final crop of blackberries from which we made jam and the mirabelles,small yellow plums,and small green wild apples provided a source of fruit to bottle.Sweet chestnuts,after you had pricked your fingers as you collected the "spiny green hedgehogs" eventually gave up their contents and dreaming of Christmas.still far away,I savoured the thought of the roasted delights in front of the yule fire.The final task before heading for home was to fill a couple of old hessian sacks with rich brown well matured leaf mould from the woodland floor,a wonderful organic fertilizer which was free.Cramming as many small dry branches on top of the sacks in the boot and we headed for home, happy with what nature had generously given to us.Exhausted,but we would eat well from the gathered fruits,be warm from the gathered wood and the leaf mould,well rotted, would give a boost to next year's crops.

****

"If you don't at first succeed ,try,try and try again"

****

Nana and I,with the rest of the congregation spilled out of Saint Faith's Church and headed home up Tribe Road,the clouds in the darkening sky stood out against the red sunset,the portent of less pleasant weather conditions in the coming days.The short journey over,I went in the door and stood in front of the glowing embers of the fire,still alight from when we had gone out,it just needed "banking up" to bring it back to life.Having switched on the little bakelite,battery powered radio,checking there was enough charge in the heavy glass cells,we settled down to listen to the music furnished by the Light programme.Nana,meanwhile,scolded Grandad,who had fallen asleep reading his paper,for letting the fire"run too low"whilst we were out, headed to the scullery to warm up the milk for a cup of hot cocoa.In no time at all she headed back with the drink,carrying a couple of digestive or butter osborne biscuits for me to dip in it."Drink it up",she said."an early bed tonight you've a big day ahead of you tomorrow",It was now September and this "big day" had been talked about all through the summer,preparations for it had accelerated in the last weeks and did little to allay my slightly bewildering fears.School was rather a daunting prospect,who would be there,would I know anyone,why couldn't Nana come with me.As I washed and brushed my teeth in the chill of the scullery,then stood in front of the fire pulling on my flannel pyjamas and dressing gown I could feel the anxiety building up,my concern for the unknown growing.Was I going to be alright,what was going to happen and was I going to be left alone?I slowly climbed the stairs,knelt to say my prayers,then climbed into bed,when I woke up tomorrow I needed to be "grown up",it was the first day on the road to being an adult.On the chair next to the bed,the blue enamel candlestick shone its light over a pile of neatly pressed and folded clothes.A white short sleeved shirt,grey flannel short trousers,vest and pants,short sleeved woollen jumper,tie,long grey socks and a pair of homemade elastic garters.Next to the fireplace downstairs was a pair of polished black lace up shoes and hanging on the back of the door a black belted, gabardine raincoat,in case it was needed.As I knelt and said my prayers,climbed between the white crisp sheets,pulled up the blanket and eiderdown,then restlessly tossed and turned I was fearful as to what tomorrow would bring.Eventually slumber took over and after a fitful night's sleep it was time to rise,that all important day had arrived which would set me on the path to whatever would unfold on life's journey.Reluctantly washing and dressing myself,the tie proving,even after much practice,a most difficult task,downstairs I went.Breakfast was already on the table but although I was hungry I had no appetite and only picked at the porridge,even though Fussells condensed milk was on offer and ignored the toast put before me.Having got down from the table I laced up my polished black shoes,a task I had practised all summer,as I had also done with my tie.A comb was suitably wetted to get my hair to lay down,sometimes not in the most hygienic way,a neat side parting put in it,always on the left and a final brisk dressing down with the clothes brush. I picked up my shoe bag and checked the contents,we couldn't afford a leather satchel so the home made shoe bag constructed from an old curtain and elastic was the best we could do.For a we lad it wa quite heavy as it contained not only my plimsolls,but an apron,a little pencil tin with its

contents of a pencil,small white rubber emblazoned with the word"Eraser" and a metal pencil sharpener.I was five years old,I was as ready as I could ever be and reluctantly,tightly gripping Nana's hand we ventured out on the short journey to Leesland School in nearby Whitworth Road.The walk was mostly uneventful and we soon arrived at the school gates,the only interruptions were from younger nervous figures,like myself, clinging to mum or grandma's skirts desperately seeking reassurance.As the school gates drew closer the more confident of the new intake entered the busy enclosed playground,whilst a few tearfully still clung to their chaperones in the forlorn hope that this experience was just a bad nightmare!!Through the black painted gate and railings,under the shady boughs of the giant horse chestnut trees,we traversed the tarmac playground towards a group which was forming near the school building. The established classes were queuing already with their teachers having assembled when summoned by the bell,chattering stopped,silence descended and in an orderly fashion.they filed obediently into the classrooms.As we entered into a wide corridor we were shown into a changing room furnished with benches and coat racks,each child was shown where to hang their bags and having changed from our outdoor shoes into plimsolls,we said our final farewells to the mums,accompanied by the odd tear,and proceeded with our new teacher to our classroom.The classroom had a very high ceiling and was heated by a huge coal fire and had at one end a blackboard standing on a wooden a-frame easel.The windows were high up and being small we were unable to see out,the lights on long cables hung down with industrial lamp fittings and illuminated the rows of wood and

iron framed desks.These heavy brown wooden desks had sloping tops which opened to reveal storage for your school items..In the rail at the top was a groove to hold your pencils and wooden handled,nibbed pen and a hole to hold a ceramic inkpot,which monitors would fill, from a large glass bottle of blue ink,Parkers,Stephens or Quink,The desks had iron frames and the seats folded up so you could stand up when the teacher entered the room for registration,a requirement and a sign of respect.There were definite signs of past use from the ink stains,attempts to engrave ones name and an occasional Arrow chewing gum,well chewed and then stuck underneath the desk.On the wall were large paper charts,the alphabet,times tables and later the adornment of our very own efforts as our artistic talent was put on display for all to view.Board rubbers,ink bottles,a globe and even slates,chalks and counting frames stood on various shelves.Here we were,the future was ours but where would we go,what was the next ten or fifteen years going to lead us to.

****

''The darkest hour is the one before dawn''

****

By the end of,1958 Christmas as we knew it in my very early years had changed dramatically in many ways.We were living at a bungalow in Masten Crescent,backing onto what was a marshy wilderness with mature trees,brambles and an abundance of wildlife.From the little copse the bird life I had only seen in the countryside was suddenly in our back garden.Woodpeckers,bullfinches,coal tits,chiffchaffs arrived almost daily and the bird table in winter was a twitchers delight,grey squirrels could be seen swinging from the top of the Victoria plum tree and a hedgehog could be heard on the driveway outside my bedroom window at night.However apart from this it was not as pleasant as before dad had remarried.It was not long before he erected a large heated greenhouse,this time growing cucumbers and tomatoes,not for Mr Shepherd,but for his own Wavy Line grocers shop in Rowner Lane.All of dad's time was spent working,and my step mothers constant attention to my half brother was less than pleasant,I still spent a lot of time at my Nana's but as she became older Christmas was "celebrated" more at Masten Crescent,and less with her.Christmas Day started with breakfast,we were.not allowed to have any presents till after dinner,on the pretence that if we did dinner wouldn't be cooked in time.The morning was spent listening to carols being sung on the radio,until eleven o'clock when Dad set off for Drift Road Clanfield to collect Ernest and Agnes Taylor,stepmothers parents,who would have dinner and tea with us before being returned home.After dinner we would open our presents from the pillow case which had supplanted the stocking as presents grew in size.Whatever,it had to be completed by three'clock,the time of the Queen's Speech,silence was expected and we sat with a cup of tea,in my case lemonade, to watch the yearly spectacle on the newly bought television set.It was little more than a box on four pencil thin legs,a sliding door covering the screen when not in use,but it was at that time the best available although only black and white and very susceptible to "interference".As the speech unfolded "Grandad" Taylor would puff on a distinctive smelling Santoy cheroot,a wiry gentlemen of small stature he always had a smile on his lips and a twinkle in his eye.His wife sat next to him had a prominent jaw and was a larger person always dressed in heavy woollen skirts and knitted jumpers.A round of board games,tea with ever popular sherry cream trifle,the only acknowledgement to alcohol accepted in the house,and something I was not allowed to partake of,making do with jelly and blancmange.By eight o'clock it was time to leave in order to get back to Clanfield,the night was"crisp and even" a frost starting to creep into the air on a very clear and starlit night,the stars twinkling like diamonds on an inky background.The car was bitterly cold,we had travel blankets covering our legs,the car boot filled with the unwrapped presents that had exchanged hands earlier.Street lamps were throwing very little light on our route and the headlamps of the car on full beam did not much of a better job illuminating the road ahead.The car,a Hillman Minx, turned into Rowner Lane,passing the parade of shops heading towards the only lamp posts at the junction of Rowner Road.Turning sharp left.within yards the lights had rapidly disappeared,on both sides were fields,as we headed towards Newgate Lane we strained our eyes to see what little could be seen in the faint yellowish glow,NewgateLane,as we turned into had a little light from the Christmas lights in the few houses where it commenced and I took the opportunity to count the trees as they popped up in the front room windows.Apart from this and an apologetic glow from HMS Collingwood provided by a large star of white electric bulbs there was nothing until we joined the Fareham Road.It was like a ghost town the number of cars on the road would not amount to more than a dozen on the entire journey.Climbing out of Wallington to cross to Boarhunt cresting the hill was magical,the twinkling stars added to by the white frost that had started to coat the roadside grass,sparkling as it was picked out by the car headlights.Passing through the farm at Boarhunt Church the cows in the open byres appeared as black and white ghosts in the shadowy darkness,on towards the twisting lanes leading to Hambledon the rural public houses,The Horse and Jockey,Chairmakers Arms and eventually the birthplace of cricket,The Bat and Ball all came from the shadows with an inviting glow from their doors and windows,nevertheless devoid of revellers.Travelling down the long sweeping road into Clanfield we crossed into Drift Lane and opened the door to a chilly interior,but a very warm welcome from Rufus an extremely excited golden cocker spaniel.Once unloaded,without further ado we said our farewells and climbed into the car to return home and the possibility of encountering exciting encounters on the journey home.

****

''Be thankful for small mercies''

****

Dad turned the car from the unadopted gravel lane back onto the main road,or rather a country lane,the start of the journey back home.We crossed the road leading to Clanfield village and headed up the hill.I was now in the front of the very chilly car sat forward on the edge of the hard seat my hands clutching the edge of the front screen my legs covered with a travel blanket to try and keep warm.As the car breasted the hill in the distance were the welcoming lights of The Bat and Ball public house,adjacent to the site of the first cricket match.The lights became closer and closer,the night so clear the surrounding fields were swathed in a silvery moonlight,the sky twinkling with millions of tiny stars.Turning left around the bend at the junction a long straight road led into Hambledon village.On the wide grass verges amongst the piles of chippings snuggled little rabbits,not all however as it should,they would wander blindly into the road or stare blankly at the headlights,many suffering from the affects of the merciless cruel virus myxomatosis.We drove through the village,the road deserted of both people and vehicles,the only tangible movement that of the coloured twinkling of the lights on Christmas trees in the little paned windows.Heading down the village main street it was a reminder of the carol"how still we see thee lie,above thy deep and dreamless sleep the silent stars go by"it was a vision that has remained with me for ever.Leaving the street,passing Snowdrop Cottage and Hartridges mineral and soft drinks factory we took a right fork towards World's End,the Chairmakers Arms and Boarhunt me peering intently ahead and above.Many occasions I would be rewarded by the ghostly outline of a white barn owl flapping and gliding across the hedgerows in search of a meal to satisfy its hunger on the cold frosty night which was to become even colder.Onwards to The Horse and Jockey before turning to Boarhunt,passing the high sandy banks which lined the road providing the ideal spot to see a vixen,her piercing yellow eyes flashing in the car lights as she turned her head and ran for cover.A few more rabbits appeared and a fleeting glimpse of the white rump of a fallow deer disappeared quickly into the roadside tracks.Inevitably the excitement of such a long day soon took its toll and by the time we had crested the hill above the church and farm at Boarhunt I had fallen into a slumber. I roused as we turned into the drive at Masten Crescent,stumbled sleepily from the car,so much so that my confusion would see me head in the wrong direction,A steady hand guided me back to the front door,once inside as if second nature,my eyes heavy and half awake,I manouvred myself from my clothes and with chattering teeth into pyjamas warm from them being wrapped around a blue rubber hot water bottle.Finally I snuggled into my bed and into

222

oblivion.

"Pride always comes before a fall"

Once I was about twelve Dad had has his shop in Rowner for a few years and with very little competition the Wavy Line shop used to do quite well.I was always discouraged from going into the shop,for what reason I don't know but a quick wave as I went by was about all the contact I had.The only time this would change would be if my stepmother had been pressed into a shift and there was nobody in at home,which was just around the corner,on those occasions I was allowed to sit in the stockroom as long as I didn't move.All my childhood I was never allowed to be at home on my own and even when there spent nearly all my time behind a closed bedroom door unless I had a very good reason for coming out.If dad,my step mother and brother went shopping,I would be ushered out and told what time I was allowed to return,fortunately I had a few friends who I was able to go to visit or meet with,but it was always made clear that they were not welcome to visit.Every day neatly suited commercial travellers would visit the shop to take orders for the goods they sold,many only responsible for one or two products.Tobacco salesmen would take your order and then go to their car and draw the stock from the boot,orders placed in single packets not large cases and some packets were of only five cigarettes.Similarly,bread,rolls and cakes,the white coated van driver would arrive and be given an order that he then picked from his van at the same time taking away any items not sold the previous day.greens were the local bakery from Hardway,their sliced loaves,branded Nuloaf,later Mothers Pride was wrapped in a waxy paper,the wrapper colour advertising the thickness of the enclosed slices.sale or return was a commonplace practice for these type of fresh items and even newspapers and magazines were treated the same way right up till present times.another salesman would provide cooked meat,pies and sausages from a blue and white Millers van.A Birds Eye van operated by a company called Kinghams would deliver your frozen food order,the amount being enough to fill the display freezer as there was no backup storage.I remember at times,after a freezer breakdown weather like kings for a few days.Sides of smoked or green bacon would be delivered by Harris's a specialist company or more often by the blue and grey lorries of DBC[the Danish Bacon Company],the driver dressed in white wearing a white pill box type cap.The bacon would be boned,cut up and sliced on a red Berkel bacon slicer with a huge blade,all of which was operated by hand.nothing was wasted even the bones sold for soup,the small pieces and damaged rashers sold for bacon puddings.The ham joints were hand carved and displayed on white china stands,the ham bones sold to make pea and ham soup,even the scrap pieces from the various meats sold for a penny or two.Because of these practices wastage of food was rare,provided it wasn't "off" or mouldy it would be used and even when mouldy the green would be scraped off,"it won't kill you" we would be told.It has to be remembered that at this time as corner stores developed into infant supermarkets that started to sell everything that the predominance was still   trade shops,butchers,bakers,greengrocers,florists,newsagents,tobacconists ll were the first choice for the traditional places to buy from.

****

"Its as the crow flies"

****

Every Monday morning,having spent most of the weekend perusing The Grocer magazine and updating the buying and selling prices of groceries using Shaw's directory,the pricing bible for the small local shopkeeper,the representative would arrive from IKC.This well established company Iven Kelletts and Child,provided a wholesale delivery service having been bombed out during the war,due to its location adjacent to a fuel depot.Dad would have prepared a basic order which would be added to when he was made aware of any special deals or offers that might be available.Once placed the representative would adjourn to a local red phone box to ring the order hrough to his head office.On occasions he would return to the shop to advise us of non availability of an ordered line and enquire as to if we required an alternative.We now had to wait until Wednesday morning for the arrival of the large orange-brown lorry,logo emblazoned on the size,the brown overalled driver armed with a clipboard on which he had the delivery sheet.Alighting from his cab he opened the unlocked doors and proceeded to pull the items required to the back edge of the lorry.All assembled he would jump down,carry the boxes into the shop and place them on the floor,then removing a pencil from behind his ear he would check the delivery under the watchful eye of the staff.No tail lifts,trolley,simple manual labour.The last thing the driver did before leaving was to hand us a pack of printed advertising leaflets which would become my task to deliver later that day.

****

"Thou shalt not take the Lord's name in vain"

By the time I had arrived home from school it was time to get changed pick up the two hundred and fifty shiny leaflets,but before I could deliver them I had to stamp the leaflets with I&G Dewane,101 Rowner Lane.After all the customer needed to know where the offers could be purchased,to me they were of little interest.It didn't take long with a rubber stamp and an ink pad and once done and the leaflet drop completed it was worth five bob in my pocket,unfortunately only once every four weeks.It didn't seem a huge amount but it managed to provide enough money for sweets with a little bit over to save.I always started in Masten Crescent before moving into Rowner Lane,walking up paths and being careful to close the gates to prevent the residents complaining to Dad and me incurring his wrath before moving on to the naval estate.It wasn't particularly easyas although the married quarters had grassed front areas it was always expected for me to walk up and down the concrete paths and not on the grass,even though it was in places worn down from children playing.Alleyways giving access to the rear of the properties sometimes provided surprises when a barking dog would hurtle after me and left me frozen to the spot,happy to see the owner arrive to take it back in.The letterboxes were not always easy to open,the low ones gave me back ache,some of the others pinched fingers and doors left ajar the leaflet just got thrown.In fine weather it wasn't too bad but when wet by the time I had got to the last deliveries it was akin to looking like chewed paper where they had been in my hand so long.I walked up Mansfield Road,halfway down St Nicholas Avenue,it seemed to take forever the rain would drive down the roads due to the openness of the road layouts,the water would drip of my forelock,my shoes would get wetter and wetter,becoming more encrusted in mud from my shortcuts across the grass.Water ran down my neck and cuffs,it was a fair certainty that nobody would come out to chastise,although one or two windows were vigorously banged and fists shook.If it was a dark night,with ineffective street lights,many of which didn't work it was easy to stumble over a child's abandoned toy,dropping the already wet leaflets or slipping up.Like all leaflet drops some houses received more than one,several dustbins were suddenly inhabited,anything was tried to end the discomfort quicker,all the time aware that if Dad found out I would be in trouble,it was not unknown for the last thirty leaflets,folded in my coat pocket to find their way into a rubbish bin at Gosport Ferry on my way to school the following morning.Dripping wet I would go back to the shop,by now he was there and would dip his hand in the till and hand me two half crowns,if I was lucky as a bonus I might be given a foil wrapped penny bar of Cadbury's milk chocolate

****

"MONEY is the root of all evil"

****

Growing up in the fifties was a wonderful time,much of it directly or indirectly connected to the phrases and sayings my Nana used.With this in mind I consciously left till last the above phrase.My life experienced the loss of my mother,grandad and nana,the birth of a half brother and the appearance of a stepmother,but overwhelmingly the lack of a real relationship with my father,who was obsessed with the pursuit of wealth.Whether it due to a poor upbringing in rural Ireland at the time of the first world war I do not know,in the fifties asking questions about theses matters was taboo.Dad was hard working,self improving and a gambler,all ways in his eyes means to more money.He was a strict disciplinarian,a fanatical supporter of right and wrong.His loss of his wife,my mother,I believe was part of the reason,due to the circumstances as to why we never always so eye to eye.The pursuit of money as a source of improvement presented any close relationship as almost impossible,no close family meant only very limited communication.Outwardly dad was the epitome of a first class father but in house the truth was far different.I loved dad,you nearly always do but I just wish that he hadn't seen money as the ultimate means to happiness.As somebody said to me,he would have seen success as being the richest person in the graveyard.Sadly my memory is of an individual who found it difficult to have a deep relationship and saw money as the means to achieve the answer.

L - #0401 - 011220 - C0 - 210/148/12 - PB - DID2967691